Living i

God's Plan for you to

Eddie Snipes

A book by:
Exchanged Life Discipleship

Copyright © 2014 by Eddie Snipes and
Exchanged Life Discipleship

http://www.exchangedlife.com

ISBN: 978-0692206331

Contact the author by visiting http://www.eddiesnipes.com or http://www.exchangedlife.com

Table of Contents

Growing by Revelation

Ephesians 1:17-19

[17] That the God of our Lord Jesus Christ, the Father of glory, may give to you the spirit of wisdom and revelation in the knowledge of Him,

[18] the eyes of your understanding being enlightened; that you may know what is the hope of His calling, what are the riches of the glory of His inheritance in the saints,

[19] and what *is* the exceeding greatness of His power toward us who believe, according to the working of His mighty power.

Let me begin this book by revealing to you a secret. You are blind. So am I. Not one of us can fully see our faults or the areas in which we suffer lack. There are areas where we struggle with a known weakness, but that is merely the tip of the iceberg of your human nature. Below the surface are many faults that are holding you back.

To put this into perspective, look at the relationships you have around you. Is there anyone in your life that has a fault that bothers you? Perhaps someone who acts selfishly, or has habits or mannerisms that annoy you? Does your spouse, family member, or co-worker have a personality quirk that is bothersome? Perhaps something that creates a conflict simply because they cannot recognize what they are doing. When you point it out, they deny it or point at your failures.

Do you know what the most common cause for divorce is in the United States? Adultery? Abuse? No. The number one reason for divorce is irreconcilable differences. It is when two people are letting the little annoyances get under their skin, and over time, the frustration is all they see. Both sides are pointing at the little things the other person is doing that drives them crazy.

The same problem plagues nearly every strained relationship. Breakdowns in workplace relationships are usually caused by someone getting on the other's nerves. In church, fightings are nearly always the buildup of frustrations of little annoyances. "Joe always...", or "Sue never..." Then the accusation is that someone interrupts, doesn't speak to me, has to be first, jumps into someone's business, dominates the group, and the list goes on. Then when someone tires of Joe or Sue, they either lash out or show some sort of rejecting behavior, and conflict escalates.

So what on earth does this have to do with understanding our life in the Spirit? These things are evidences that we are drawing from the flesh. The flesh is incapable of seeing itself in an honest light but has no problem seeing the flaws in others. Let me give an example. While driving on the highway, I passed a car with a bumper sticker which read, "Hang up your phone and drive." When I passed the car, the driver had her face in the mirror putting on makeup.

That's human nature. Your carelessness needs to be rebuked, but mine is justified. Your behavior is hazardous, but I see nothing wrong with mine. Your behavior annoys me, but mine is okay. Look at someone who annoys you. Think about the times when you wondered, "How can they be so blind?"

Now here is the secret. That person is you. Just as 'that person' cannot see their faults and can't see how it bothers others, you can't see your faults and how it bothers others. Some personality types are more subtle and don't grate as much on people's nerves, but we are all in the same boat.

The more we see through the eyes of the Spirit, the more we begin to recognize how helpless we are to change our lives without the promise we read in Ephesians above. The more we recognize our need, the more we'll understand the helplessness of others. According to the scriptures, the revelation of God is given to us so we can believe and allow Him to transform us according to His power. Without that revelation, we remain blind to both our need and His power.

The truth is that you will not even recognize your need until after you begin experiencing the power of the Spirit. And herein lies the problem of human relationships and human methods. I can tell you how you need to change, but because you are incapable of seeing beyond your human point of view, there is no way for my words to reveal your need to you.

You can tell me my faults and the things I do that bother you, and I'll be bothered at your judgmental attitude toward me. I'll begin wrestling with my own feelings of defensiveness, and I'll believe I'm not that bad. It's you who need to quit demanding everything to be perfect for you. Right?

Even if someone doesn't say it, they are thinking about how you are doing the very things you are accusing them of. And the most frustrating people think that everyone else is the problem. We've all known people who were their own worst enemies. They bring out the worst in others because they create conflict. Yet that person will believe everyone is against them. How is this possible?

All of us are that person to varying degrees. Now here is another secret. You will not recognize your faults until you have already grown out of them. A counsellor can help people cope, but they cannot change a person's ways of thinking and personal perception. They may be able to do some good by shifting their focus onto healthier things, but this is usually short-lived, and even when it's successful, that success is limited.

There is a reason why God said, "As the heavens are higher than the earth, so are My ways higher than your ways and My thoughts are higher than your thoughts."

We look at the problem and try to fix it. Or try to get the other person to fix it. But as a friend of mine likes to say, "What you think is your problem is not your problem. And that's the problem."

We are attacking the symptom and trying to fix ourselves and others by strengthening the very thing that is causing our problem – the flesh. Take to heart **Romans 8:5-6**

> [5] For those who live according to the flesh set their minds on the things of the flesh, but those *who live* according to the Spirit, the things of the Spirit.
> [6] For to be carnally minded *is* death, but to be spiritually minded *is* life and peace.

This is the reason why the Bible uses words like 'repentance'. We think of repentance as apologizing to God, asking for forgiveness, and promising never to do something again. But the word repentance means, "To change the mind."

If your mind is set on the things of the flesh, you will reap the things of the flesh. If you are trying to fix yourself by patching up the flesh, alter how the flesh thinks, or doing anything by human effort, you are empowering your fleshly mind to lead your life. The result is ALWAYS a mind set on the flesh. It can do nothing but produce the works of death in our lives. This book will go into how to understand the life of flesh verses the life of the Spirit in detail. For now, realize that if you are trying to empower the flesh to overcome the flesh, you will be ruled by the flesh. The flesh cannot overcome itself.

You cannot see yourself clearly; therefore, you certainly cannot fix yourself. And the person who annoys or frustrates you is in the exact same position as you are. Your behavior will not change or be recognized until you outgrow that old way of thinking. Consider **1 Corinthians 13:11-12**

[11] When I was a child, I spoke as a child, I understood as a child, I thought as a child; but when I became a man, I put away childish things.
[12] For now we see in a mirror, dimly, but then face to face. Now I know in part, but then I shall know just as I also am known.

When did the Apostle Paul put away childish things? Did he put these away so he could mature into a man? No. When he became a man, he put away these childish things.

This is you and I. When we look at ourselves in the mirror, we have a clouded judgment. Even the person who is down on themselves has pride. If you don't believe that, commit a wrong against them and see if they don't say, "How dare you do this to me?" When we look at ourselves, we are completely limited by our self-perception.

When God reveals Himself to us, it is in a way that calls us to be transformed into His likeness. Then as we are transformed, we clearly see the areas of our lives that are no longer compatible with our current level of maturity. It is then that we put these things away, for they now appear childish to us.

If you have been a Christian for any length of time, you may already see evidence of this in your past. Some things you did, said, or believed now appear silly – maybe even embarrassing. Yet at the time you thought it was wise.

A child may believe in childhood fantasies, but an adult living in a fantasy world is disturbing. When I was six-years-old, I felt tough strutting around with a cap gun hanging from my belt and a sheriff star pinned to my shirt. I would have felt like a fool wearing that outfit when I was sixteen.

No one had to tell me to put my cap gun away. As I matured, childish things began to fall from my life. No one told me I was too old to play with GI Joe. My parents never had to say, "Eddie, now that you're in high school, it's time to put away the Romper Stompers."

Yet this is how we approach spiritual life – both for ourselves and for others. We want to say, "You shouldn't act this way," yet we leave them in preschool and wonder why they keep acting like preschoolers. No, if they become men and women of the faith, they will put away childish things. If we mature in Christ, our selfish attitudes will begin falling away. The behavior that mountains of criticism could not correct, I will gladly put out of my life once my maturity outgrows that childish thing.

No one will have to tell you how to correct your behavior. When that area of your life reaches adulthood, you will put it away because it appears childish to you. As you grow in the Spirit, even areas people don't view as childish will fall from your life because they are incompatible with where you are going – and growing.

This is the purpose of this book. Though you will never be perfect on this side of eternity, as you reach ahead toward perfection, the joy of what God continuously reveals to you will

Growing by Revelation

make worthless things appear worthless, and reveal the value of eternal things.

Just as the toy you thought was priceless now appears worthless, so will it be in your spiritual life. And as you grow into maturity, the joy of fellowship with God and others will flourish and become the fragrance of your life.

Now let's stop and reflect for a moment. Think of something you struggle to correct in your life. It might be anger, bitterness, a negative attitude, lust, a habit, or any number of things. Why do you think you struggle? It is because your value system is broken. I get angry because I value my ego or control of my world more than I value others. I am greedy because I value money and things as if they have lasting worth. A habit is something I value more than my willpower can resist.

How have you tried to correct this in the past? Probably by trying harder, finding accountability partners, or some form of personal effort or commitment. Why hasn't it worked? It's because at the moment of temptation, you value that desire more than your commitment.

I once heard someone give this advice to an addict, "Just don't do it." To that person I say, "You also should just stop doing the things that emerge from your own weaknesses." Just don't get angry. Just don't get annoyed. Just don't worry. It doesn't work because it can't work.

Here is my advice to you who may be struggling now. Though I am not advocating indulging in harmful behavior, I also would say, "Stop trying to fix yourself." It is not your role to fix the flesh. The flesh cannot be fixed, as we'll see from the scriptures in the following chapters

The Bible gives the following promise, "Walk in the Spirit and you will not fulfill the lusts of the flesh." The lusts of the flesh is not just sensuality, but any craving of the flesh. That is what lust means, an intense desire. It could be the flesh's desire to retaliate for a wrong. It could be anger, greed, self-righteousness, pride, or anything the flesh desires to protect itself or gratify itself.

Until your life in the Spirit becomes reality, the false reality of your fleshly desires will have more value than their true worth. God is NOT asking you to fix yourself. God is inviting you to walk by faith with the promise that He will take you out of the broken life of the flesh and into the life of the Spirit – the place where the flesh has no power. Read this wonderful promise, **Micah 7:19**

He will again have compassion on us, And will subdue our iniquities. You will cast all our sins Into the depths of the sea.

Who subdues our sins? It is God who subdues the flesh so we can rejoice in the freedom we have in the Spirit. The man or woman who walks in the spirit is free from sin. Sin can only occur when we are drawn back into the mind of the flesh. Yet even then we have the promise that God casts the sins that bind us into the sea of His forgiveness, and He stands as our guard. Our sinful flesh cannot sneak past His guard. He subdues it and we rejoice in this life in the Spirit we have been given.

Living as an overcomer is achieved by walking in the Spirit. Not only does God subdue the sins you already see, but as you grow, you'll be in a constant state of discovery of childish things as you grow into deeper maturity. Instead of groveling in defeat, we pluck them off like burrs and flick them away.

But you can't see these childish things until after you have outgrown them. Until then, you are either empowering the flesh to pursue lusts, or empowering the flesh to challenge the righteousness of God with your own flesh-based counterfeit righteousness.

Stop trying to fix yourself and others. Start growing in faith and leave the childish things behind!

Discussion Questions

Review Romans 8:5-6. If we look to ourselves to change, are we in the flesh or the Spirit?

What results can we expect?

Do you believe you have faults you cannot see?

How do we or others overcome the fleshly ways of thinking we can't see?

Do childish ways prevent us from growing?

What keeps the Christian in immaturity?

How does my value system affect both what is seen as important AND what is a weakness in my life.

Review Ephesians 1:17-19. How do we discover our need?

How do we find the power to change?

The Promise of the Spirit

One thing that separates good doctrine from false teaching is found in **1 Corinthians 13:13**

> And now abide faith, hope, love, these three; but the greatest of these *is* love.

When everything in scripture is reduced to its simplest element, it will teach or affirm either faith, hope, or love – or all three. Fear is not a valid doctrine, for the Bible says that anyone who fears has not yet been perfected in love. God's perfect love expels fear, according to scripture.

Doctrine that creates doubt, hate, fear or anything fashioned out of these things is false teaching. These things are outside of Christ, and anyone in Christ has escaped the bondage of the flesh. Those who haven't escaped from fear and doubt are missing the work of God. Let's let the Bible explain. **1 John 4:18-19**

> [18] There is no fear in love; but perfect love casts out fear, because fear involves torment. But he who fears has not been made perfect in love.
> [19] We love Him because He first loved us.

Fear is a powerful tool for manipulating others, but a terrible tool for building up the body of Christ. Fear and doubt merely reveal that a person is not yet walking by faith. Teaching that centers upon fear reveals that a person does not yet understand the power of the Spirit and the gift of God.

Never fear failure. Never fear that God is angry or disappointed with you. God knew your failures before you were born, and He has fashioned the events of your life to lead you out of failure and into the victory that overcomes the world, our faith.[1] In the flesh, failure is impossible to avoid. This is true even if we

---

[1] 1 John 5:4

The Promise of the Spirit

think we are doing good. In the Spirit, victory is a guarantee – even if you have just blown it in the flesh.

Stop fearing your sins and start trusting in Christ and the promise of God's Spirit. Trust in the promise that sin will fall away as you mature into spiritual adulthood. Don't trust in doubt. Don't trust in fear. Trust in Christ. He is your victory. When you blow it in the flesh, you've merely seen firsthand what God said would happen. In the flesh, you are always in defeat.

The hardest thing for Christians to understand is that good works done in the flesh is still sin. Jesus said that many will come to Him to present their good works. They will show Him how they preached the word, fed the poor, did wonderful works, and even performed miracles – all in Jesus' name. Yet Jesus says, "You are a worker of sin."[2]

How can good deeds done in Jesus' name be called an act of sin? From the human perspective, this seems preposterous, but let's look at it from the perspective of the work of Christ. The Bible says that Jesus fulfilled the law and all of its requirements on our behalf.[3] Jesus became sin on our behalf that we might become the righteousness of God in Him.[4] Jesus said that this is the work of God, that we believe on Him.[5] The love of God and salvation through His love is a gift that cannot be earned.[6] This gift is received by faith in Him.[7] Finally, to count the New Covenant as valueless is worse than breaking the law of the Old Covenant.[8]

When we try to make ourselves righteous, we are discrediting the gift of righteousness God has given us through Christ. So then, our works becomes our declaration of independence from the work of Christ. It is to say, "Jesus, what you did is not sufficient. I can do it better," or, "I must complete what Jesus could not do." It

---

[2] Matthew 7:23
[3] Romans 8:4
[4] 2 Corinthians 5:21
[5] John 6:29
[6] Ephesians 2:8-9
[7] Galatians 3:14
[8] Hebrews 10:29

is to make my righteousness become a rival to the righteousness of God given to me.

The second thing the church has a difficult time accepting is that our sins become irrelevant once we begin walking by faith. Sin is in the flesh. We'll examine this in detail in a later chapter. Once we are in the Spirit, sin cannot follow. Nor can condemnation, guilt, shame, or anything of the flesh. Those things are of the flesh, and the Bible promises, "If you are led by the Spirit, you are not under the law."[9]

Sin has no power in the Spirit. In fact, if you look at the commands to keep the law, the Bible says that it is written to those who are under the law, but if you are of faith, you are no longer under that legal system.

To the carnal mind, this is absurd. To say that the requirements of the law no longer applies is to make light of sin, right? It's a license to sin, right? Let me ask it this way. When you walk into a nursery, do you feel tempted to hide toys under your shirt and sneak them out? No? Why not? It's because you no longer have the mind of a three year old. You don't need a parent or nursery worker checking your pockets to make sure you aren't taking the toys. There are no rules preventing you, you just no longer have that mindset.

This is why people don't understand the life of the Spirit. To the spiritually immature, no longer being under the law sounds like giving sin free reign. But to those who are walking in the Spirit, calling grace a license to sin sounds foolish. Or as the Apostle Paul stated it, "How shall we who have died to sin continue to live in it?" He concludes his answer of this absurd accusation in **Romans 6:6-8**

> [6] knowing this, that our old man was crucified with *Him*, that the body of sin might be done away with, that we should no longer be slaves of sin.
> [7] For he who has died has been freed from sin.
> [8] Now if we died with Christ, we believe that we shall also live with Him,

---

[9] Galatians 5:18

Certainly, if your value system is still being drawn from the flesh, freedom looks like an opportunity to sin. Yet when we start walking according to the promise of life, we understand that our old nature is dead and removed. It's in the grave. Why would we want to wallow in the corpses? That's ridiculous.

What the church has been doing is preaching in the flesh to the flesh, and then trying to use the rules of the flesh to restrain the flesh. And we can't figure out why this doesn't work. If someone doesn't understand life in the Spirit, they will view spiritual matters through the flesh. Since it is plainly evident that the flesh cannot restrain itself, and most church members live according to the flesh, it only makes sense to institute rules and regulations that will bind the flesh. The rules are not creating people with thriving spiritual lives. It only seeks to restrain.

The church has given up on the promises of God, "You shall not fulfill the lusts of the flesh," and are trying to compensate by teaching people that they should shackle the flesh. Then Christianity falls from freedom and becomes a new form of bondage. Then we are surprised that people are casting religion aside and trying to find freedom through liberal theology or complete abandonment of the faith.

When the Bible says, "Where the Spirit of the Lord is, there is liberty,"[10] but Christians are feeling oppressed by the church, something is wrong.

Fear, guilt, and condemnation are the only tools that can restrain the flesh outside of true faith, so the church has centered its doctrines around these three points. Yet the Bible says we should be centering around faith, hope, and love. Do you see the conflict? If our three main doctrines are in contradiction to the Bible's three main doctrines, do you think Christians will truly experience the abundant life Jesus promised?

You will never experience liberty and discover a thriving life of faith until you believe the promise that the body of sin has been done away with in Christ, and you have been set free from sin.

---

[10] 2 Corinthians 3:17

While the disbelieving Christian says this is freedom to sin, God has declared, "No, you have been set free from sin. If you have died with Christ, believe that you are alive in Christ."

If you have been born as a new creation through Christ, you are now alive with Christ. Believe this truth and walk as someone who is alive – not someone who is still fighting to overcome death.

What would happen in the church if we quit preaching, "Look at your sin," and started preaching, "Look at the new life you have in Christ?" If people started believing in the promise that they are the righteousness of God in Christ, would they live differently? If instead of trying to use the body of sin to fight sin, we started believing the promise, "Walk in the Spirit and you will not fulfill the lust of the flesh," would it have an impact? Does preaching that we are the righteousness of God in Christ excuse sin? To make such a claim is absurd – even blasphemous.

The 'look at your sin' doctrine simply does not produce fruit. It can't. The best it can do is inspire you to try harder, and you'll have success only as long as the fear of failure is greater than the temptation to sin. And that temptation might be stress. When the pressures of life become greater than your strength to hold your temper, what do you think is going to happen? When you fail, where will your focus be drawn? The fruit of trying harder is greater guilt and frustration. But the fruit of the Spirit is the manifestation of the glory of God in your life.

Take this promise to heart and meditate on it. **Galatians 5:16-18**

> 16 I say then: Walk in the Spirit, and you shall not fulfill the lust of the flesh.
> 17 For the flesh lusts against the Spirit, and the Spirit against the flesh; and these are contrary to one another, so that you do not do the things that you wish.
> 18 But if you are led by the Spirit, you are not under the law.

Do you believe this promise? Now let me ask another question. Where in the Bible do you see any type of promise that if

The Promise of the Spirit

you try harder, commit more, and do more righteous acts you have the promise that the lusts of the flesh have no power?

Read the above passage again. The flesh's desires are incompatible with the Spirit. The desires of the Spirit are incompatible with the flesh. These two will never agree. If this is true, how will your human efforts produce godliness, righteousness, or any other fruit of the Spirit? Can you really trust in your flesh to make you acceptable to God? Can it conform your behavior to a spiritual standard? Maybe a spiritual standard acceptable to other people of the flesh, but it can never make you like Christ.

All human effort is of the flesh. Anything that depends on what I do for God is a work of the flesh. Anything that is based on faith in Christ, faith in God's love, or faith in the hope of God's promises is of the Spirit. It's all about faith, hope, and love – and each of these is focused on what has been given to us through Christ and received by the Spirit.

Let me share another promise that I hope will become a reality in your life by the end of this book. Look at **John 7:38-39**

> 38 "He who believes in Me, as the Scripture has said, out of his heart will flow rivers of living water."
> 39 But this He spoke concerning the Spirit, whom those believing in Him would receive; for the Holy Spirit was not yet *given*, because Jesus was not yet glorified.

The people of God from the beginning of the Old Testament to the day of Pentecost could not obtain this promise. But you have obtained it – even if you don't know you have it.

Those who are born through the Spirit have also received the Spirit. If the Holy Spirit is within you, so is the fountain of living waters. This not only waters your soul, but it also pours life into the church and the culture around you. Yet if we clog our lives with the flesh, there will be no flow of the Spirit. And the Spirit will only flow in the life of those who understand that their life is in the Spirit and walk by faith in the Spirit. It is God who decided to make faith (trusting in Him) the only barrier or conduit in the Christian life.

Faith is the conduit that flows into your life. Faith in the flesh flows the things of the flesh into your life. What many people call faith is actually trusting in the flesh. Are you the shield for your faith, or is faith your shield? Are you upholding faith, or is faith upholding you? Faith in God flows the things of the Spirit into our lives. Even if we are trusting in the flesh, it doesn't change the work of God. It only changes whether we are walking in that work.

In the Old Testament, there is a story about a king named Nebuchadnezzar. God raised him up to rule the world at that time. When this king became lifted up with pride, God warned him that if he failed to recognize this was a gift from God, the Lord would humble him.

Sometime later, Nebuchadnezzar stepped onto his balcony and saw the wonders of his kingdom. "Look what I have done," he said. An angel rebuked him and he lost his sanity. He thought he was an ox. In a short time, he was grazing in the fields instead of dining in the palace.

Just because this king thought he was an ox, acted like an ox, and fed like an ox, was he an ox? No. He was just as human during his insanity as he was during his glory days. Seven years later, the Lord revisited him and restored his sanity. He praised God and acknowledged that all was the work of God's hands, and soon he was living as the king in the palace again. The only thing different between the man grazing in the field and the man sitting on the throne was what he thought of himself.

Unlike Nebuchadnezzar, God has not caused us to think we are beasts of the field, but our enemy has. The only thing different between the victorious Christian and the one driven by the beast of his flesh is what he or she understands about their true identity in Christ.

If you believe the lie that you are your flesh, you will graze on what the flesh craves. If you believe the promises of God, you will live as a receiver of His goodness. Certainly you can live like a spiritual pauper. Other paupers will tell you how to dumpster dive for the things that look good to paupers, but are repulsive to the children of the kingdom. What's worse is that instead of saying, "I

The Promise of the Spirit

want that too," Christian paupers will rebuke you for the audacity of thinking you can live like a child of the king.

You *are* a child of the king, not because of anything you can do, have done, or will do. Even the dumpster diving Christian is a child of the king, but as long as you, and they, don't believe in what God said He has given, you will never live like a child of the kingdom.

Eternity has already begun. For those who understand the spiritual reality of our Kingdom, this is already a reality we can begin discovering and experiencing now. Jesus even stated this in **Luke 17:20-21**

> 20b He answered them and said, "The kingdom of God does not come with observation;
> 21 "nor will they say, `See here!' or `See there!' For indeed, the kingdom of God is within you."

The time is coming when the reality of the Kingdom will be seen with our eyes, but we don't have to wait – it is now. You are in the kingdom now, and the weaknesses of the flesh have no power against the life in the Spirit. You are already there. Stop living like a defeated Christian and start walking in fellowship with your Father now. He delights in you, and that is the meaning of Christianity. God wants you to experience fellowship with Him now. And God does not permit sin to interfere with that relationship.

The best part is that sin is not your concern. Your weaknesses, failures, and flesh are not for you to fight. It is God who has promised to subdue your sins, reveal His strength in your weaknesses, and produce every spiritual gift in your life. All He asks is that you walk by faith.

These three things remain – faith, hope, and love. Faith in Him, His works, and His word. Hope in His promises knowing they are reality. Rest in His agape love. God is love, and we must believe in the love He has for us. If you believe in fear, you are denying yourself the relationship given to you through Christ, and you are denying God the joy of seeing you enjoy the gifts of His love.

If you are a parent, you know the joy of seeing wonder in your children's eyes. As a parent, I delight in seeing my kids get excited at a present I have given them. What happens at the party of the child who pouts and refuses to enjoy what they have been given? The child deprives themselves, and the parent is disappointed that they couldn't have the joy of seeing their smiling faces.

What if an adopted child comes out of an abusive home and is afraid to accept gifts? That child is missing out on what is rightfully theirs, and the parent grieves that the joy is missing.

Unlike human relationships, God's gifts don't spoil us, for we receive through a spiritual nature that is born of God. It's only when we fall back into the flesh that the gifts and relationship is lacking.

As we press ahead, keep in mind that God gave His promises so that we could experience the fullness of Him, and so He could experience the joy of expressing His love toward us. Faith, hope, and love – these are our promises from God.

Discussion Questions

Review 1 Corinthians 13:13. Should true teaching affirm faith, hope, and love?

Why does most teaching communicate fear? Is there a place for fear-based teaching? Why or why not?

Read Matthew 7:22-23. How can someone do good works in Jesus' name and be called a worker of lawlessness (or sin).

Why would Jesus reject the very works He said His disciples would do?

Read Hebrews 10:28 - 29. Which is worse, disobeying the law of the Old Covenant, or counting Jesus' sacrifice as insufficient?

According to the Bible, how is the sin of the flesh defeated? Through my resistance to sin, or through walking in the Spirit?

Why does God fill His word with promises to us?

If Jesus promised that any who believed on Him would have the Spirit flowing out of them like living waters, why don't we see this as part of the normal life of Christians?

Why does God make faith (trusting in Him) the only qualification for receiving the things of the Spirit?

Body, Soul, and Spirit

A once-popular radio teacher scoffed at the concept of people having both a soul and a spirit. Having grown up under the teaching that the soul is our spirit, and our spirit is our soul, I readily agreed with him. That is until I was challenged by the scriptures that rebuke this belief. One of these passages is **Hebrews 4:12**

> For the word of God is living and powerful, and sharper than any two-edged sword, piercing even to the division of soul and spirit, and of joints and marrow, and is a discerner of the thoughts and intents of the heart.

It may seem like a minor thing to confuse the spirit and the soul, and though one does not have to understand this to have faith in Christ, it does affect how we approach our spiritual walk. Confusing the soul and the spirit adds to the misunderstandings that cause people to attempt to live out their faith through the soul, i.e. human effort. How do we learn to receive from the revelation of God's word if we can only process through the human mind? After all, the Bible tells us that our natural minds cannot understand the things of the Spirit.

This misunderstanding also causes confusion when we read passages that say, "The soul who sins shall die." Does this mean when we sin, we are back under condemnation? What about the passage from 1 John that states, "Whoever is born of God cannot sin, for he has been born of God?" If I commit a sin, does this mean I am not a Christian? How can the Bible say that we have the mind of Christ, but then warns that we can be carnal (or fleshly) minded?

Let's explore the body, soul, and spirit and see how the Bible sheds light on this topic.

Review the passage in Hebrews above. Why does the word of God pierce deep within us to divide the soul from the spirit? We are not talking about God's Spirit in this passage, but man's spirit.

Keep in mind that the Bible says that faith comes by hearing the word of God.[11]

When the word is preached, the Spirit of God does a wonderful work in our hearts. Before we came to Christ, we had a spirit that was dead.[12] It was inherited from Adam and is the source of our sin nature.[13] In the Old Testament, God promised our new birth in Christ. Look at **Ezekiel 36:26-27**

> [26] "I will give you a new heart and put a new spirit within you; I will take the heart of stone out of your flesh and give you a heart of flesh.
> [27] "I will put My Spirit within you and cause you to walk in My statutes, and you will keep My judgments and do them.

When God promised a heart of flesh, He is not referring to the fleshly heart we see discussed in the New Testament. God is saying that He will remove the heart that is hardened by sin, and replace it with a heart that is tender toward righteousness. This heart will be based on a new nature given through Christ that draws its direction from the Spirit instead of from the flesh (or old sinful nature).

Notice something very important in this passage. Our new spirit will be in fellowship with God's Spirit, and He will cause us to walk in obedience.

The Old Covenant was based on the law forcing man to do what was against his nature. The New Covenant is based on the promise of God giving us a new nature that is of God and causes us to act by the desire of righteousness from within.

The Old Testament promises that a time will come when God will indwell the believer, purge out the old sinful nature, and create a new spirit with a new nature. This is the gospel message. Jesus calls this being born again. We are born through Adam with a sin nature, but in Christ, we are born again into a new nature whose

---

[11] Romans 10:17
[12] Ephesians 2:5
[13] 1 Corinthians 15:22

life is in Christ. A great passage that helps explain this is **Colossians 2:11-14**

> [11] In Him you were also circumcised with the circumcision made without hands, by putting off the body of the sins of the flesh, by the circumcision of Christ,
> [12] buried with Him in baptism, in which you also were raised with Him through faith in the working of God, who raised Him from the dead.
> [13] And you, being dead in your trespasses and the uncircumcision of your flesh, He has made alive together with Him, having forgiven you all trespasses,
> [14] having wiped out the handwriting of requirements that was against us, which was contrary to us. And He has taken it out of the way, having nailed it to the cross.

The Old Testament circumcision was actually a symbol of what God was about to do within the heart of man. Just as the animal sacrifice was a foreshadow of what God would one day do through Christ, the ordinance of circumcision was also a foreshadow of what God would one day accomplish in us through Christ.

This is why the word of God is called the sharp two edged sword that divides the soul from the spirit. It is the method God uses to circumcise our hearts. The soul was ruled by the sinful nature of our old spirit, God divided the two, cut away the old nature, and replaced it with a new nature. Just as the flesh of a male child was cut away in circumcision, the flesh of each believer has been cut away when we receive the promise of Christ by faith. That fleshly nature is cut away, and only then can we enter into God's covenant of promise.

Why then do we still have a tendency to sin and how do we overcome our fleshly ways of thinking? This is the purpose of this book. Understanding our life in the Spirit is the key to walking by faith. Notice that the soul is divided from the spirit. That's the work of God. The old nature has been taken away, but the flesh remains.

Here is how our old life operated in the flesh. The body of flesh demanded its cravings to be satisfied. This begins at birth. A baby cries when he or she is hungry. Their demand is met when they are fed. When the body is uncomfortable, the baby cries. A diaper is changed, covers are provided, or they are given attention. It's the parent's responsibility to meet these needs – both physical needs and emotional needs.

As we grow from an infant, we demand more. Our flesh craves satisfaction from the world around us. We want toys, attention, candy, and a child will demand more and more unless consequences create more discomfort than what they crave.

Even in adulthood, we are looking to our bodies for satisfaction. Every desire is gratified, or we set on a quest to find out how we can gratify it. Our sense of self-worth is based on what we feel, what we possess, and how we can create glory for our egos.

Our body of flesh is how we experience the world around us and how we gratify our needs and desires. Our soul is our personality. It's our mind and emotions. Our spirit is our inner most being. It gives life to our bodies, or as the Bible says, the body without the spirit is dead. Or as Genesis 2:7 states, "God breathed into Adam's nostrils the spirit of life, and he became a living soul."

Some translations use 'breath' and 'being' instead of 'spirit' and 'soul'. The Hebrew word 'neshamah' means 'spirit'. In Genesis 2:7 (man became a living being), the Hebrew word which is translated as either 'being' or 'soul' is the word 'nephesh', which means soul, or self-life. The Hebrew word is not 'spirit' but 'soul'. Self-life is the focus of the soul.

Who are we? If our identity is drawn from a sinful nature, self is a sinner. If our identity is drawn from the spirit given through Christ, we are called the righteousness of God in Him. [14]

What this helps us to understand is that in our life before Christ, our body served a sinful nature whose desires were based on selfishness and personal gratification. The body's cravings were based on a sinful nature and the soul was subjugated to the body

---

[14] 2 Corinthians 5:21

to act out in ways that pleased the body and the sinful nature behind it. The unredeemed soul is always subject to the body.

In the new life we have, the reverse is true. We have a new nature, born of God, in fellowship with God, and whose desires are the same as God. Yet the body has a lifetime of having its cravings satisfied, and it is unwilling to deny itself. It cries out like the infant who has never matured beyond learning how to demand what it wants. It demands to be gratified and tries to subjugate the soul to pursue the old sins that once fed it. So now we have an internal conflict. This is the subject of **1 Thessalonians 5:23-24**

> [23] Now may the God of peace Himself sanctify you completely; and may your whole spirit, soul, and body be preserved blameless at the coming of our Lord Jesus Christ.
> [24] He who calls you is faithful, who also will do it.

Let's bring in another passage that helps shed more light on this idea of complete sanctification. The Corinthian church struggled with sin among its members. The Apostle Paul begins his letter to these fleshly minded Christians by saying, "To those who are sanctified in Christ Jesus."[15] Paul then addresses sin in the church and draws the comparison between who they are verses who they were. He goes on to list the sinful lifestyles prevalent in the culture around them. Now let's pick up in this conversation by looking at **1 Corinthians 6:11**

> And such were some of you. But you were washed, but you were sanctified, but you were justified in the name of the Lord Jesus and by the Spirit of our God.

You were washed? You were sanctified? You were justified? These are all past tense because they are accomplished facts. They aren't sanctified because of what they do or didn't do. This is evident because Paul addresses many sins in the church – including rebuking those who were visiting prostitutes.[16] He calls them

---

[15] 1 Corinthians 1:2
[16] 1 Corinthians 6:15-18

Body, Soul, and Spirit

sanctified, and then four verses later he rebukes them for sexual sins and warns them of the consequences of sin.

How can they be sanctified and still in sin? Their spirit is sanctified because it is in Christ. Let's revisit **1 John 3:9**

Whoever has been born of God does not sin, for His seed remains in him; and he cannot sin, because he has been born of God.

Before we dig into this passage, let's also look at **1 Peter 1:22-23**

[22] Since you have purified your souls in obeying the truth through the Spirit in sincere love of the brethren, love one another fervently with a pure heart,

[23] having been born again, not of corruptible seed but incorruptible, through the word of God which lives and abides forever,

This is why the Bible says, "You were sanctified." Your spirit is in Christ, born of the Holy Spirit, and eternal. Its life is in God, of God, and by God. Nothing in God can sin. It's impossible. Your new nature is sanctified, for it was born in that state. Sanctified means to be set apart for God. But look at this passage from **Romans 8:10**

And if Christ is in you, the body is dead because of sin, but the Spirit is life because of righteousness.

This is written to those who are in Christ and who have the Spirit of Christ in them. In the Spirit, you have life because of God's righteousness, but your body is still corrupted by sin.

Before Christ, the corrupted nature fed its desires to the body. The body of flesh demanded the soul to pursue sin. Since our will had nothing other than a sinful nature to draw from, it always sided with the body and the soul was subject to the desires of the body. The only restraints we had were the cultural standards and the fear of consequences. And sometimes those were also not enough to deter sin.

Now that we are in Christ, the body is still dead because of sin, and it demands to be gratified, so it does what it has always done. It attempts to subjugate the soul to serve its desires. The will draws from the mind and if the mind is in the Spirit, the body is denied its demands. If it's in the flesh, it submits to the body. Consider **Romans 8:6**

> For to be carnally minded is death, but to be spiritually minded is life and peace.

If we understand the body, soul, and spirit, this passage makes sense. How can a Christian be carnally (or fleshly) minded? Because it is drawing from the flesh. The mind can be focused on the Spirit or on the flesh. Then it will draw its values from its focus.

The spiritually minded Christian will live according to the Spirit, renew their minds, and use their soul to bring their bodies under obedience. Or as Romans 6 explains, "Do not submit your bodies again to sin, but as someone who is alive from the dead, submit your body as an instrument of righteousness."

The average Christian tries to use their flesh to accomplish works of righteousness. Then every deed is of the flesh, and the more the flesh is in power, the more it will rule the mind. This is why church people can act very un-Christ like while doing very religious things. Righteousness cannot be accomplished by what we do. It is not good deeds working from the outside in. It must be the work of God from the inside out.

The only way to live as an overcomer is for our spirit to be the focus of our soul, and then our soul can bring the body under subjection. Only then can we submit our bodies as instruments of righteousness. Since the Bible says the body is dead because of sin, and that sin dwells in our bodies,[17] the body cannot do good unless it is first brought under submission to the spirit. The body is never the source of good, but it can be used as a tool for righteousness.

This is why our hope is in God to sanctify us completely, body, soul, and spirit. Complete sanctification is when the body is subject to righteousness because the soul is drawing from our spirit, which

---

[17] Romans 7:20-23

Body, Soul, and Spirit

is drawing from the mind of Christ, which is the Holy Spirit within us. Every Christian has the Holy Spirit and the mind of Christ – even if they are completely ignorant of this reality.

Is it necessary to believe this in order to be a Christian? Certainly not. However, those who do not understand this truth will live a frustrated Christian life. The only way to bring the body under subjection is to first be in the Spirit.

When the flesh demands its way, if we are depending upon our human efforts, we have already lost the battle. It's only a matter of time before the works of the flesh begin to emerge. If we believe our soul is our spirit, then we have no understanding by which we can draw from the Spirit when sin wars against our minds to bring us back under subjection (see Romans 7:23).

When we understand how sin wars, we can then overcome through the life we have in Christ. Or as the Bible says, "Lest Satan get an advantage over us, for we are not ignorant of his devices."[18] Let us equip ourselves with what God has provided, and walk by faith in the life we have in the Spirit!

---

[18] 2 Corinthians 2:11

Discussion Questions

Do you believe the soul is different than the spirit? If so, what is the difference?

Read John 4:24. Can we have fellowship or experience worship through our soul? Explain.

What is the purpose of circumcision? How does this apply to the life of faith?

Why does the Bible call us sanctified, and then say, "That you may be completely sanctified, body, soul, and spirit?"

Can our spirit be corrupted by sin? Why or why not?

Can our soul be corrupted by sin? Why or why not?

Read Romans 6:13. How do we prevent the body from being a tool for sin?

How do we present our bodies as tools of righteousness?

Can we do good deeds and still be outside of God's righteousness? Explain.

The Mind of Christ

Let's begin this chapter by looking at **1 Corinthians 2:9-11, 14-16**

9 But as it is written: "Eye has not seen, nor ear heard, Nor have entered into the heart of man The things which God has prepared for those who love Him."

10 But God has revealed them to us through His Spirit. For the Spirit searches all things, yes, the deep things of God.

11 For what man knows the things of a man except the spirit of the man which is in him? Even so no one knows the things of God except the Spirit of God.

...

14 But the natural man does not receive the things of the Spirit of God, for they are foolishness to him; nor can he know them, because they are spiritually discerned.

15 But he who is spiritual judges all things, yet he himself is rightly judged by no one.

16 For "who has known the mind of the LORD that he may instruct Him?" But we have the mind of Christ.

There are a few things I want to bring into focus from this passage. This chapter will discuss five main principles from the above scripture:

1. The things man cannot see or imagine has been revealed to us.
2. No one knows the things of God except the Spirit of God.
3. The natural mind cannot receive the things of the Spirit.
4. The things of God can only be discerned through the Spirit.
5. We already have the mind of Christ.

The things man cannot see or imagine has been revealed to us.

Keep in mind this is written to the Christian and is an instruction on Christian principles. The main point is that we have spiritual discernment because of the Spirit of God within us, and the believer has the power to see what the world cannot see. What's more, the Christian who is approaching the scriptures and the Christian life from the perspective of their natural mind cannot see or receive the deep things of God.

The law can be observed through the natural mind. Even the unbeliever can read, "Thou shalt not kill," and understand that it's wrong to kill. But the naturally minded man cannot understand the spiritual principles that the law directs us to discover, and he certainly cannot understand the things of faith, or the spiritual world that we now live by.

If the Christian is ignorant of the Spirit and how He interacts with our spirit, we will approach the Bible from the natural mind and miss the greater things that can only be received through the Spirit. That person cannot know or receive the things of God, for God's revelation to us can only be discerned through the Spirit.

The way of truth is foolishness to the world. Not only that, a life of walking by faith is foolishness to most churches. The reason is that most Christians teach from the natural and the church is focused on the natural. That's why people say things like, "Grace is a license to sin." To a life viewing religion through the natural mind, rules, regulations, and church restrictions are the only ways to keep people in check. How can someone know not to sin unless the church is standing over them pointing out every known sin and warning people not to commit these?

The spiritual man looks at both the Christianized version of the law and the call of sin and says, "Why would I who have died to the flesh and now have life in Christ want to return to the flesh and continue to live according to its way of death? Why would anyone who has escaped death want to return to it?"[19]

The natural mind can't understand this, so it attempts to conform people to a mock-spiritual standard where we are the

---

[19] Romans 6:2

The Mind of Christ

foundation of our behavior instead of founding our behavior on the finished work of Christ.

The natural mind waits for heaven. The spiritual mind is already walking in the kingdom. The natural mind says, "If I work hard enough, one day I'm going to have a reward in heaven." The spiritual mind says, "God is my exceedingly great reward."

The natural mind says, "I must do the right things to please God so I am acceptable to Him." The spiritual mind says, "I am accepted because I am in Christ. Without faith it is impossible to please God, but because my hope and trust is in Him, I am pleasing and can rejoice in my daily fellowship with Him."

The natural mind looks at the scriptures and says, "I must force myself to spend time in the word." The spiritual mind says, "I can't wait to open the word to discover what God has prepared for me to find."

One works to obtain, the other rests in Christ knowing they have been given all things. The natural says that believing the previous statement will create apathy, but the Bible says that understanding grace creates a people zealous for good works.[20]

Let's look at the spiritual verses the natural to see this truth. In Luke 18, a rich young ruler came to Jesus and asked what must he do to obtain life? He trusted in the law, so Jesus gave him the full measure of the law. Jesus mentioned the command to love your neighbor as yourself.[21] The young man claimed that he had been fulfilling this since his early youth.

Really? Then why was he rich and his neighbor poor? Jesus said that if he was to fulfill this perfectly, he must sell all he had and give it to the poor. This religious, moral, upstanding citizen could not do it. He walked away sorrowful. Jesus pointed at his love for the things of life and explained how it would be easier for a camel to pass through the eye of a needle than for the rich man to receive eternal life. With people, this is impossible, but with God all things are possible. And Jesus is about to prove His power to do the impossible.

---

[20] Titus 2:11-14
[21] Matthew 19:19-20

People's mouths gaped. Was all hope lost for people such as this successful, but moral man? If you have money, you can't be saved? Then an interesting thing happens. In the very next chapter, Jesus meets another wealthy man. This man was filthy rich, morally bankrupt, and increased his wealth by using the corrupted Roman tax system to sap money from every person in his city. He was so hated that when Jesus walked by, the people shoved him back. All he wanted to do was get a glimpse of this man everyone was talking about, but he was denied.

You've probably guessed by now, his name is Zacchaeus. After many failed attempts, Zacchaeus ran ahead and climbed a tree. Jesus, the one who was supposed to be the most godly man in Israel saw this vile sinner and said, "I will dine at your house today."

Oh the horror. In that culture, to dine with someone was a declaration of friendship and acceptance. The leaders had already criticized Jesus for dining with prostitutes and drunkards, but now He was going to dine with the pinnacle of sin in that culture – the thieving tax collector.

After an evening of fellowship, an interesting thing happened. Without any command or prompting by Jesus, Zacchaeus said, "I want to make things right with my neighbors. I am going to give my goods to the poor and pay back four times the amount I have cheated out of anyone."

What? The conscienceless immoral thief was going to do the very thing the moral, upstanding ruler of impeccable character could not do? One tried to use the flesh to accomplish what human nature could not stomach. The other found grace and it gave him the desire to do what the law could not accomplish.

This is the natural verses the supernatural. If you approach your faith through human reasoning and personal effort, you are robbing yourself of the power of God. When God reveals Himself to you, your spirit will rejoice in the will of God, and you will do what your natural abilities could not accomplish. You will desire what your natural mind once tried and failed to do for God. Your desires for the things of the Spirit will grow, and the things of the

The Mind of Christ

flesh (even habitual sins) will lose their appeal. Sins will fall away because they become incompatible with your spiritual mind.

Best of all, you will understand the deep things of God and rejoice in the transforming power of His word. And you don't have to make yourself do anything. Life in the Spirit rejoices in the ways of God. You will be following your desires, but because you now value what is good, those desires will be pleasing to God. That's when you experience the promise of Psalm 37:4, "Delight yourself in the Lord and He will give you the desires of your heart."

No one knows the things of God except the Spirit of God.

Let's revisit the passage that introduced this book. **Ephesians 1:17-19**

> [17] That the God of our Lord Jesus Christ, the Father of glory, may give to you the spirit of wisdom and revelation in the knowledge of Him,
> [18] the eyes of your understanding being enlightened; that you may know what is the hope of His calling, what are the riches of the glory of His inheritance in the saints,
> [19] and what is the exceeding greatness of His power toward us who believe, according to the working of His mighty power.

Your eyes must be enlightened by God's Spirit. Knowledge is vital, but knowledge without revelation is nothing more than religious philosophy. The Bible says that knowledge itself puffs up, or makes us proud. This is plainly evident in many churches. Anyone who has been in church for long has probably met someone who was puffed up with knowledge. To them, knowledge makes them elite, and the Bible is used to beat people down or demand submission to themselves and/or their doctrinal positions. Knowledge through the Spirit is not so.

Now let's bring points four and five into this discussion since they are inseparable from the revelation knowledge of the Spirit.

- **The things of God can only be discerned through the Spirit.**

- **We have the mind of Christ.**

One thing that emerges in the life of someone receiving knowledge through the Spirit's revelation is a sense of wonder. Rather than being puffed up, that person begins to realize that there is a world of understanding yet to be explored. Every revelation is a new world of knowledge. That's when we begin to grasp the Apostle Paul's comment, "Anyone who thinks he knows anything doesn't yet know anything that he ought to know."[22]

Each discovery reveals more of the depths of God. Then we understand that each new revelation merely introduces a new depth of God to explore – and as the scriptures state, "Oh, the depth of the riches both of the wisdom and knowledge of God! How unsearchable are His judgments and His ways past finding out!"[23]

Instead of being puffed up with pride, we begin to discover how little we know, and how much God desires to reveal.

Now here is one of the most mind-blowing promises of scripture. We have the mind of Christ. If you are born into God's kingdom, you have the mind of Christ. The mind of Christ is not your mind, but the mind of the Spirit that resides in you, who are the temple of the Holy Spirit.[24] This means that everything God knows is within you, waiting to be discovered. And it is only discoverable by those who learn to walk in the Spirit.

There are some who teach that your spirit is the Holy Spirit. This is a complete misunderstanding of scripture. What's more is that it misses the joy of fellowship. Remember the passage from Ezekiel we read earlier? God promised two things. He promised to create in us a new spirit, and He promised to place His Spirit within us. The Holy Spirit is uncreated, but our new spirit began at our new birth in Christ.

This is what you have. God is within you, and your spirit has communion with the Holy Spirit. And the Holy Spirit is eager to

---

[22] 1 Corinthians 8:2
[23] Romans 11:33
[24] 1 Corinthians 3:16

The Mind of Christ

reveal the mind of Christ to you. Yet most people are so focused on the natural mind that they remain ignorant of the spiritual mind we have by promise.

Even though all God has for you is already yours, it remains undiscovered until you begin walking in the Spirit and exploring God. Something has to bring the things of the Spirit into our human minds. This is what is meant by revelation knowledge. Revelation knowledge is not the creation of a new truth, but it's God revealing to us that which has always been – His knowledge and His life.

This is revealed through the word. That is why the Bible says faith comes by hearing the word of God. Hearing the word puts our focus on the truth being revealed, and by faith we enter into God's invitation to believe and receive. Countless people use their natural minds as the source of revelation, and are deceived by the flesh, spiritual wickedness, and pride. Yet the Bible commands we test the spirits to see if they are of God. [25] This is also true when we are learning something that contradicts what we have been taught to believe. We should be like the people of Berea – receive the word and then test it against the scriptures to see if the teaching is true. [26]

The word of God was rejected by the law-focused Jews of Paul's day, but instead of rejecting what they didn't understand, the Bereans (who were also Jews) listened and then dug into the scriptures to see if it was true. They were then called 'honorable' by God. We see the same war today. Traditional beliefs that have excluded many powerful truths of God have become an idol so that people reject anything that challenges their sacred traditions. Yet some are noble-minded and will allow traditions to be challenged and are willing to study the word to see if these things are true.

We are also told that anyone who thinks they have a revelation (prophecy) is subject to the word of the prophets whom God used to pen the scriptures. [27] Let's go back to the verse that began this chapter – **1 Corinthians 2:9-10**

---

[25] 1 John 4:1
[26] Acts 17:10-11
[27] 1 Corinthians 14:32

⁹ But as it is written: "Eye has not seen, nor ear heard, Nor have entered into the heart of man The things which God has prepared for those who love Him."

¹⁰ But God has revealed them to us through His Spirit. For the Spirit searches all things, yes, the deep things of God.

If your background is like mine, you've probably been incorrectly taught this passage. From an early age, I was taught this was the hope of heaven. Eye hasn't seen, nor the ear heard, nor has it entered into the heart of man what God has in store for those who love Him. This is our heavenly reward, right? No. Read the whole thought in this passage. These things have been hidden from the natural mind. Those who are not in the Spirit cannot think, hear, see, or imagine the depth of what God has for those who love Him – but – they *have* been revealed to us!

God has revealed to you the things no human can even imagine. Even Christians can't imagine the depth of God's truth, even though it has already been revealed to them. Yet that revelation does not come from the intellect, but the revelation of the Spirit. This is not merely the hope of heaven, but your life now. Do you believe the word?

This takes us to the third main point of our introductory passage, **The natural mind cannot receive the things of the Spirit**. If you are approaching the Bible and your spiritual life through the natural mind – the intellect – you are incapable of perceiving the deep things of the word of God. You will be stuck in surface Christianity. This is where the vast majority of Christians reside. Superficial faith is all that surface Christianity can discover.

In your spirit, you already have the mind of Christ. Your inner man is in constant fellowship with God, even if your natural mind is distracted with this world, fleshly desires, and even religion. This is even true for religions that claim the name of Christ.

As you learn to walk in the Spirit, your soul is brought in line with your life in the Spirit. Then the deeper things of God being revealed to your spirit flows into your soul, and your mind can then receive revelation knowledge. Let's examine **Romans 8:5-6**

The Mind of Christ

⁵ For those who live according to the flesh set their minds on the things of the flesh, but those who live according to the Spirit, the things of the Spirit.
⁶ For to be carnally minded is death, but to be spiritually minded is life and peace.

If your life is according to the flesh, a fleshly mind is all you can live by. A mind drawing from the flesh is the natural mind. Natural in the sense that it is rooted in the mindset of the old nature. So even if you try to walk in obedience, read the Bible, pray, and do church things, you are still bound by the limitations of the carnal mind. You may get small glimpses of God, but you can never go below the surface to discover the deep things of God.

The mind in the Spirit lives by the Spirit, discovers the things of the Spirit, and grows into maturity so the deeper things can be received. And as those things are received, we mature all the more and the discoveries are endless. You will never receive more than your spiritual life has grown enough to receive.

Since most people are focused on what they are doing for God, they are blind to the promises of what God has given them. As long as we look in the wrong direction, we cannot see what is being given to us freely by God. Anything that is not based on faith is the wrong direction. Are you trusting in yourself, your works, your religion, or your efforts? Then you are not walking by faith. Faith is always trusting in God. It is trusting in what God has said, what God has done, and what God has given. Meditate on **Hebrews 11:6**

But without faith it is impossible to please Him, for he who comes to God must believe that He is, and that He is a rewarder of those who diligently seek Him.

How do we please God? By what we do? Don't do? No. Only faith pleases God. When you believe God, you will seek Him diligently, and then you'll discover all He has for you, and as you learn how to receive, your life will be continuously transformed.

Then works and spiritual fruit can do nothing but emerge as you grow in the faith.

You won't diligently seek the things of the Spirit until you believe God. Do you believe you have the mind of Christ? Do you believe you are the righteousness of God in Christ? Do you believe you are a partaker of God's nature? That is what faith is all about. Then you will seek what you know has already been given. Remember, Jesus said, "Seek first the Kingdom of God and His righteousness, and all these things will be added to you."[28]

Jesus didn't say that we should seek to become righteous. Nor did He say to seek our own righteousness. We are commanded to seek God's Kingdom and God's righteousness. And why are we seeking these? Because all has been given to us. The only righteousness we can have that God will accept is His own righteousness given to us as a gift of His love (ie grace). Jesus also said, "It is your Father's good pleasure to give you the kingdom."[29]

It gives God pleasure when you receive His kingdom. It is already given, now all God asks is for you to seek Him as you believe that He has given you all things. That is the beginning of what it means to walk in the Spirit. Seek because God wants you to find. When you are seeking Him, God will not allow you to miss His promises. It is His desire to see you receiving the promise. God's promise was given because it is His desire for you to receive.

You already have the mind of Christ. Seek the things from above so they become reality in your life here below.

---

[28] Matthew 6:33
[29] Luke 12:32

The Mind of Christ

Discussion Questions

Who followed God's word more closely, the rich young ruler, or Zacchaeus the tax collector?

Why didn't Jesus command Zacchaeus to keep the law or part with his possessions?

Why was Zacchaeus able to do what the law-keeping rich ruler could not do?

How does God reveal deep truths to us? How do we become a part of what God is revealing?

How can we have the mind of Christ if we are limited in our understanding?

Does God reveal the deep things only to clergy (Pastors, priests, church leaders)?

Will God give revelation without the word/Bible?

If someone has a revelation that contradicts the scriptures, is that a new revelation?

How do we know if someone's revelation is of God?

If something pops into our mind, is that a revelation? How do we know?

Is it possible to discover the deep truths of God without first building on the foundation of the elementary truths of scripture?

How does the mind of Christ make it to our human understanding?

What prevents this from occurring?

Does reading your Bible make you spiritually minded? How do misinterpretations of scripture happen?

Explain what it means to seek God's kingdom and righteousness.

It's all about Faith

It is impossible to walk in the Spirit without faith. In fact, walking in the Spirit *is* walking by faith. Until you understand what it means to trust in God's grace, you will remain mired in personal effort and mere religion.

Let me stop for a moment and define grace. The Bible tells us that God is love.[30] No other description is given for the essence of who God is. The Bible tells us that God is Spirit,[31] and then tells us that we cannot approach God through physical or fleshly methods. We worship in Spirit and truth, not through what we do in the physical. Though Spirit tells us what God is, love tells us who God is and what is His nature.

Grace is the love of God, packaged for us and given through God's many gifts. Grace appeared in the person of Christ.[32] In the same sense, grace is given to us through Christ.[33] While there is God's benevolent grace upon all people, such as the promise that God sends rain on both the just and the unjust, the gift of grace comes only to those who are in Christ. Everything God wants you to have and experience concerning His agape love comes through the finished work of Christ. These are gifts, not things we earn.

If there is one thing that prevents people from walking by faith it's this: we do not believe in the depths of God's love. Those who are in Christ have escaped corruption, sin, the law, and all condemnation. Yet most Christians live as though they are trying to obtain these by what they do. Some acknowledge that God's grace is a free gift, but then teach that we must do the right things in order to maintain those gifts. It is as if they believe God gives us gifts, but then will snatch them back if we annoy Him. Take these words to heart, **1 John 4:16-19**

---

[30] 1 John 4:8, 1 John 4:16
[31] John 4:24
[32] John 1:14
[33] 1 John 1:17

[16] And we have known and believed the love that God has for us. God is love, and he who abides in love abides in God, and God in him.

[17] Love has been perfected among us in this: that we may have boldness in the day of judgment; because as He is, so are we in this world.

[18] There is no fear in love; but perfect love casts out fear, because fear involves torment. But he who fears has not been made perfect in love.

[19] We love Him because He first loved us.

If you have fear, what does this scripture say about that? If you are abiding in love, there should be no fear. There is no fear of judgment. There is no fear of wrath. God's love is what perfects you. Therefore, if you fear judgment, wrath, or any other thing, you have not yet been perfected in love. Your focus is on learning how to abide in love. If you abide in God's love, you are abiding in God. How much simpler could God state this?

God's love transforms you into His image. You don't become like Him so you can be counted worthy of His love. Human love is conditional; God's love is unconditional. Love doesn't require you to change – it is God's gift of love that changes you. If you fall back into human thinking, you haven't been perfected by love. And the answer is given in the first verse above – know and believe in the love God has for you.

Until you believe in God's love, doubt will haunt you. You will struggle to overcome. Sin will rule you. Then the vicious cycle of fleshly minded Christianity begins. Our sins become our self-made barrier to God's love. Since it is God's love that expels sin, we can never become perfected without it. Yet we try to force ourselves to conform to our ideas of God's requirements. Though we may have moments of perceived success, because we are trusting in the flesh to overcome itself, we fall each time our human nature/flesh grows weary of forcing itself into a righteous mold.

Jesus said, "That which is born of the flesh is flesh, and that which is born of the Spirit is spirit." Our human efforts cannot produce righteousness, for the flesh, at its best, is still the flesh. Whether you disbelieve in God's ability to satisfy you and pursue the lusts of the flesh, or you disbelieve in God's righteousness and attempt to produce your own righteousness, you are in sin.

It's hard for people to accept this, but human achieved righteousness is just as much sin as sexual immorality. Both are denying Christ and trying to fulfill ourselves by human effort. Everything is a gift of God's love, or it is of the flesh. Consider this passage from **Hebrews 11:6**

> But without faith *it is* impossible to please *Him*, for he who comes to God must believe that He is, and *that* He is a rewarder of those who diligently seek Him.

Most Christians give lip service to this passage, but they don't truly believe it. If your good works are not acts of faith in God's love, they cannot please God. If you are trying to merit God's favor or earn love or acceptance in any way, it is not of faith and cannot please God. You cannot please God by what you do or don't do.

It's all about faith. Do you believe in the love God has for you? Then you will receive God's love knowing He is giving it because that's who He is, not because of who you are or what you've done. Walking in the Spirit is walking by faith.

Do you believe you are the righteousness of Christ? Consider **2 Corinthians 5:21**

> For He made Him who knew no sin *to be* sin for us, that we might become the righteousness of God in Him.

How do you become righteous? It is a gift of God. By faith, you receive this promise of righteousness. What can you do to nullify the righteousness of Christ? You can deny your righteousness, but you can't nullify the work of Christ. People can walk as deniers of Christ. It does not change who He is or what He has given, but it does not benefit any who do not walk by faith.

Is the person living for the world walking in the Spirit? No. Therefore, a fleshly minded Christian is not the evidence God's promises are insufficient. If that person is in Christ but lives for the flesh, does that change who they are?

Think about the example of the prodigal son. He abandoned his father, lived for the world, and invested his life in something that eventually led him into rummaging for food in a pig sty. Was he still a son when he was in the pig sty? When he walked away from the father, was he denied? No. All the denial came from his side, but the father longed for him to return. And once his sins drove him to the realization that the world had nothing to offer, he returned.

His plan was to become a servant, but he was never less than a son. His father never allowed him to finish his speech. While he was trying to say, "I'm not worthy to be your son," the father is calling out, "Bring a robe for my son. Put the family ring on his finger."

This is how most Christians view their failures. They believe their sins nullify the love of their heavenly Father, but all the failure is on their end. The only thing they need comes from the love of God. If the weakness of the law was the flesh,[34] it is certain that grace cannot be strong through our human efforts. If your Christian walk is dependent on you, you are no more likely to succeed than those who failed to please God in the Old Testament.

When you blow it, that only proves God true, and it reveals to you both the love of God and why faith in His promises are so important. Look at the words of **1 Corinthians 4:7b**

> And what do you have that you did not receive? Now if you did indeed receive *it*, why do you boast as if you had not received *it*?

You will never have anything to boast of. Everything you have is a gift of God, and your only role is to receive it by faith and abide in God's gift of love. Anyone who thinks they are righteous in any other way than trusting in Christ is not walking in the Spirit. Anyone who thinks they are not righteous in Christ because of their own limitations or failures also is not walking in the Spirit. One is denying

---

[34] Romans 8:3

the power of Christ and trying to accomplish what Christ has already done, the other is denying the power of Christ to defeat sin. Both are faithless. To understand this better, let's look at **2 Peter 1:3-4**

> [3] His divine power has given to us all things that *pertain* to life and godliness, through the knowledge of Him who called us by glory and virtue,
> [4] by which have been given to us exceedingly great and precious promises, that through these you may be partakers of the divine nature, having escaped the corruption *that is* in the world through lust.

The next few passages in 2 Peter 1 go on to explain that for this reason (that we are partakers of His nature), we should add to our faith virtue, knowledge, self-control, perseverance, godliness, brotherly kindness, and love.

Notice that all these things are what we add to our lives as we partake of His nature. None of these things are what we accomplish for God. Virtue means moral excellence. Do you struggle with lust or some other sexual temptation? Stop focusing on your ability or inability to be pure, and have faith in His gift of grace. Moral excellence is a gift from God's nature to your life. Lust cannot remain when God's spirit is empowering you with virtue.

Do you lack self-control in areas of your life? Has beating yourself up over your failures worked? It isn't your role to fix yourself. It isn't even your role to focus on your failure. Look to Him and receive the power of the Spirit that produces self-control. Here is the answer to your weaknesses. Look at **2 Corinthians 4:7**

> But we have this treasure in earthen vessels, that the excellence of the power may be of God and not of us.

God is not asking you to become good for Him. God has placed the treasure of His love in your earthen vessel (physical body) so you can experience victory and know it is His power and not of you.

Let me tell you something most Christians reject, but is true. God wants you to struggle with your weaknesses. God doesn't want you to succeed by human effort. That is a cheap substitute for the real thing. God allows the weakness of your flesh to overcome your life in the flesh so you look to Him and find the eternal value of His gifts. Then when you stand by grace, you know it is His power and not what you have done. It teaches you to believe and rejoice in His love for you. That is the true source of joy!

Those who think blessings are based on our love for God can never understand the depth of God's love for us. When the prodigal walked away from his father, he did not see the value of the father's love. The father loved his son enough to allow him to fail. He knew the son was going in a direction that would cause pain. I have no doubt he tried to warn his son. But until the son failed, he was convinced the world had something of value, and that he had the power to do it his way.

All the father had to do was deny his son's inheritance. The young man couldn't have left without money. Legally, the father didn't have to provide the inheritance until after his death. Yet this example of an earthly father was given by Jesus to illustrate the love of our heavenly Father.

When the young man left, the love of his father had little value to him. When he returned, he thought that love was conditional, and he was willing to become a servant just to eat food. What he discovered was that his sin against his father didn't change his father's love. His foolish choice cost him much, but when all his strength and reliance was stripped away, he discovered the depth of his father's love.

This is God's love for you. God will allow you to sin if you insist on doing so. His word warns us of the consequences of sin. He shows us how much we have in His promises. But there will be times when we sin. And one of the main ways we sin is by declaring our own righteousness as sufficient for living the Christian life. God will allow you to pursue self-righteousness. He knows your righteousness is insufficient to overcome your weaknesses, but until you believe this, God will allow you to toil in human effort. And He'll allow your flesh to war against your religious goals.

Like the prodigal son, we will keep trying to make it work as long as we are convinced the power to succeed is in us. Many Christians fall back to self-deception and hypocrisy in an attempt to cover their sins and flaws. Self-deception works as long as something big doesn't come along to knock us off our feet. At some point in life, we'll hit the famine – just like the prodigal son did. His life was working fine until something beyond his power came along. Then his desperation persuaded him to compromise his beliefs in order to survive. And that is all he did – survive. Barely.

How long did the son feed among the trash with the pigs? We don't know how long, but we do know he was willing to keep trying until he became so famished he couldn't go on.

This is your life outside of the Spirit. If you talk with anyone who has a deep understanding of grace, they are always people who have come to the end of themselves. Many times they spent years, even decades, trying to make themselves holy, but there came a time when they understood they were destitute and needed to be rescued. That is when they discovered the richness of God. But until they understood their poverty, they could not understand the value of what they have in Christ.

The sins that overthrow you today have no power in the life in Christ. They are only empowered in the life that is trying to live out their faith by personal effort. In reality, that person's faith is in themselves. It's easy to say, "God gave me grace so I can do it," but that's a lie. God's grace is what accomplishes the work. God does not ask us to do what Christ has already done.

Most churches will praise you for doing the work. When you fail, they will tell you to try harder. The focus will either be on persevering by human effort, or blaming it on unfaithfulness to God. There can be no success by personal achievement. Even if you replace a character flaw with religious busyness, you still have not done anything that has eternal significance.

God has declared, "No flesh shall glory in My presence." Not one person will stand before God and say, "Look what I did for you.

I have purified myself for you." The only answer to that is, "Why did you reject the gift of Christ?"

The Bible says that anyone who rejected the Old Testament Law was condemned. Then the Bible asks, how much worse will be the one who counts the blood of the covenant of Christ as a worthless thing?[35] When Jesus' work appears to be worthless to us, we use self-effort as an attempt to create something we think is more valuable. Most people do this out of ignorance, and that is why God allows our weaknesses to reveal our need.

It's all about faith. Your works for God cannot please Him. It is only faith that pleases God. Faith is looking at God's gift of grace through Christ and rejoicing in what God has done for us. Faith steps out of the flesh (where sin abounds) and into the Spirit to receive the gift of righteousness. A man or woman of faith says, "Sin, you have no power. I receive the righteousness of Christ." Then what more can be done to improve upon that?

Unbelief says, "I must sanctify myself for God."

Faith says, "I am sanctified in Christ."

Unbelief says, "I must be holy."

Faith says, "I am holy in Christ."

Unbelief says, "I must be righteous."

Faith says, "Christ is my righteousness."

Unbelief says, "I must get this sin out of my life so God can accept me."

Faith says, "I have been made accepted in Christ. Sin has no power in the Spirit."

Unbelief says, "I must do good works to get a reward in heaven."

Faith says, "It is God who works in me to accomplish His will and do His pleasure. I have the privilege of being a part of what God is doing."

Unbelief says, "If I do enough good things, I'll receive a crown in heaven."

Faith says, "I already have all things. I will not allow human philosophy to steal my crown or rob me of God's gifts."

---

[35] Hebrews 10:28-29

It's all about faith. It is not what you do for God, but what God has done for you. We abide in God's love, walk in His promises, and the commandments of God are fulfilled in those who walk by faith. It's impossible to walk in disobedience if you are walking by faith. It is also impossible to walk in obedience without walking by faith. And faith is not trusting in your love for God, but His love for you.

Walking by faith is walking in the Spirit.

Discussion Questions

What does the Bible mean when it says God is love?

Does sin expel God's love?

How do we abide in God?

Is God pleased by how much we work or how much we sacrifice for Him? Explain.

Can our sins cause God to disown us?

Must we drive sin out of our lives in order to receive God's gifts of the Spirit? Why or why not?

Read 2 Corinthians 4:7. Explain how this applies to your life of faith.

Will God use our sins to lead us into His righteousness? Explain.

Why do so many Christians struggle and feel spiritually inadequate?

Do commonly held beliefs and teachings prevent people from recognizing God's purpose in our struggles?

Does God love us more when we are walking by faith than when we are living through the flesh? Explain.

The Crucified Life

Romans chapter six sandwiches God's explanation of grace between two questions – shall we sin that grace may abound? Verse 1 asks this, and then verse 15 finishes the explanation of the crucified life with the question, "Shall we sin since we are no longer under the law but under grace?"

Grace, if viewed through the eyes of the flesh appears to the outsider as a license to sin. As I've stated previously, people scoff when grace is taught, and often accuse the teacher of the very thing Paul was being accused of.

Paul flows from the promise that grace abounds more than sin to the question people outside of grace will ask about grace justifying sin, and then he explains why grace can't create sin. He ends his explanation with the same question again. Then he answers by saying, "How can we who have died to sin live any longer in it?"

It is because people don't understand the crucified life that the concept of the fullness of grace seems preposterous. Of course grace doesn't make sense to the fleshly mind. If we are still alive to sin, then everything is either a license to sin, an excuse for sin, or a justification for our sins. You don't need grace to excuse sin. People with no concept of grace sin and find excuses. You and I do this more than we realize.

If I say something inconsiderate, it's because you provoked me. Right? The Bible calls outbursts of wrath, rude gesturing, and selfish behavior sin. My license to sin is my perception of a wrong done to me. Even without hearing of grace, my flesh will find a license to sin.

Grace, in the hands of the flesh, is just another tool used for self-justification. Yet without grace, the flesh still behaves as the flesh, but now we can blame grace, right? Only in my mind. In reality, my sins are never justified by what I am reacting against. No excuse can transform sin into righteousness. I can only deceive myself into feeling better about what I am doing, and human nature grasps at any justification – with or without the doctrines of the Bible.

But God has given us the gift of grace to defeat sin. One of the manifestations of God's gift of grace is the crucified life. Romans 6 unveils this truth like no other, so we are going to dig heavily into this chapter. This chapter begins by telling us we have died, and for this reason, how can we live for sin? Let's pick up in **Romans 6:3-7**

> [3] Or do you not know that as many of us as were baptized into Christ Jesus were baptized into His death?
> [4] Therefore we were buried with Him through baptism into death, that just as Christ was raised from the dead by the glory of the Father, even so we also should walk in newness of life.
> …
>
> [6] knowing this, that our old man was crucified with *Him*, that the body of sin might be done away with, that we should no longer be slaves of sin.
> [7] For he who has died has been freed from sin.

I encourage you to read the entire chapter. For the sake of space, I'll pull out the passages that are relevant to our discussion here. The first thing to notice is the purpose of baptism. It is the outward declaration of what has occurred within our hearts. Though baptism is a common practice, few people understand what they are actually testify to.

Something has died, was buried with Christ, and something new has come out of the grave. The Bible says we were crucified with Christ. Jesus died on the cross in the flesh, and the temporary body that went into the grave is not what came out of the grave. The corrupt was buried and what cannot be corrupted emerged.

Jesus compared it to a grain of wheat or corn. That lifeless looking seed is buried. It dies, and a new life emerges. The grain doesn't continue, it gives up its fruitless life and a living plant rises from the ground.

This is the symbolic example of what happens when you become a Christian. Your life of flesh is buried. You and your sins are nailed to the cross with Christ. You and your body of flesh are buried with Christ. Your new life rose with Christ. It is the work of God and nothing we did or can do. We look back 2000 years and say, "That's when Jesus died for my sins." According to the Bible, we were chosen in Christ before the foundation of the world. [36] According to Revelation 13:8, Jesus was the Lamb who was slain before the foundation of the world. In Hebrews 4:3, the Bible says that God's works were finished before the foundation of the world.

This was taught regarding those who were given God's promise of rest, but could not obtain because of their unbelief. They failed to enter God's promise – even though the work was already done and was completed before the earth was created.

Jesus didn't pay for your sin 2000 years ago. He entered into man's realm 2000 years ago to reveal the work of salvation He accomplished before the world was founded. Or as 1 Peter 1:20 puts it, "What God foreordained was manifested in these last times for you."

The same is true for your individual salvation. The work is an accomplished fact. It is so important for you to understand and believe this, for until you do, you can't enter the promise by faith and walk in the reality of what God has done for you. Just because it was finished doesn't mean we can't miss it. The Old Testament saints missed the promise, even though it was an accomplished fact.

The crucifixion of your sins and body of sin was accomplished before the world began, revealed through God's work on the cross 2000 years ago, and then revealed to you as an individual at the moment you felt God's call to receive the promise. Sin was defeated on the cross. Your body of sin was buried with Christ. You are free from sin, though until you believe enough to walk in this reality, you will live in the desert of unrest.

The Bible promises that since we died with Him, we also shall live with Him. Anyone in this promise also has the promise that death can no longer reign over him. Just as death can no longer

---

[36] Ephesians 1:4

burden Christ, you who are in Christ can no longer be bound by the body of death and sin.

Sin has no power over you. In Christ, you have been set free from sin – all sin. Sin was crucified on the cross. Your body of sin was crucified on the cross. Your old life died and now you are a new creation. At this point you might be asking, "If this is true, why do I still struggle with sin?" Let's see how the Bible addresses this very question. Look at **Romans 6:8-12**

> 8 Now if we died with Christ, we believe that we shall also live with Him,
> 9 knowing that Christ, having been raised from the dead, dies no more. Death no longer has dominion over Him.
> 10 For *the death* that He died, He died to sin once for all; but *the life* that He lives, He lives to God.
> 11 Likewise you also, reckon yourselves to be dead indeed to sin, but alive to God in Christ Jesus our Lord.
> 12 Therefore do not let sin reign in your mortal body, that you should obey it in its lusts.

Do you believe God? If so, reckon – or believe and account – yourself as dead indeed to sin. Not dead, maybe, but dead indeed. It is an accomplished fact. If you believe you are a sinner, you will live as someone trying to eradicate sin. You will then be trying to climb the hill of defeat through your own efforts.

Think back to the Old Testament people who could not enter the promise. God promised them the land. All they had to do was enter. They sent spies in and discovered there were impenetrable cities, strong warriors, and people who towered over them. They looked at the sticks and clubs they had as their only weapons. They then looked at the iron chariots and sharp swords of their enemies and said, "We can't do it."

Of course they couldn't do it. It wasn't for them to do. They were only called to walk in the works God created beforehand, and as they stepped forward, God would begin unveiling the victory of His finished work. The strongest city was Jericho. Its walls were impossible to bring down. Yet when God unveiled His work, the walls fell flat and became stairs for the people to enter into the city. God unveiled His finished work, and all they had to do is walk in it.

You can't defeat sin in your life. You can't overcome the flesh. It's not your job to eradicate sin. That is (or should I say was) God's job. Sin was defeated on the cross, and as you walk in faith, God will unveil His completed work in your life.

As long as you don't believe it is finished, you will always remain in defeat. Once the people of the Old Testament chose unbelief, God sent them back to the desert. A few decided that they could take the land by force. They were warned not to go, for no one can enter the promise unless God is calling. They tried anyway and were completely defeated. The survivors were driven out wounded and humiliated.

This is the average Christian life. When you or I decide we are going to drive out sin, we are wounded and defeated. God will not permit you to enter the promise by human effort. If you try to defeat the flesh by religious efforts, personal methods, or trying harder, even if you are sincere and praying for victory, you will not see victory. Most Christians live unvictorious lives with moments of short-lived success. This is because the victory is only through Him. Faith in Jesus' completed work is the only gate to victory.

Let's draw in another passage from **Philippians 3:12, 16**

12 Not that I have already attained, or am already perfected; but I press on, that I may lay hold of that for which Christ Jesus has also laid hold of me.

...

16 Nevertheless, to *the degree* that we have already attained, let us walk by the same rule, let us be of the same mind.

A little is lost in translation here. 'To the degree that' is not part of the original text. The words are italicized to indicate the translators added these words for clarification. The assumption is that since Paul said he hasn't attained, verse 16 must not mean we have attained. I'll explain why I believe this is an inaccurate assumption.

Throughout the Bible and in both Peter's letters and Paul's letters to the churches, scripture emphasizes that we have been given all things through Christ. We have attained these promises because they have already been given to us through Christ. Yet as we have seen in the finished work of the Promised Land, people missed the promise, even though it was already given.

Paul is looking at both the promise and the reality of his life. In order to get a better grasp on this, let's bring in two passages that may appear to be contradictory on the surface. Look at **1 Corinthians 6:11**

> And such were some of you. But you were washed, but you were sanctified, but you were justified in the name of the Lord Jesus and by the Spirit of our God.

You were sanctified – past tense. It's an accomplished fact. But now look at **1 Thessalonians 5:23**

> Now may the God of peace Himself sanctify you completely; and may your whole spirit, soul, and body be preserved blameless at the coming of our Lord Jesus Christ.

May God sanctify you completely? But we were sanctified, right? Our sanctification is an accomplished fact, but now we are being called to walk in that sanctification by walking according to the Spirit. When I learn to live by the Spirit, the reality of my spiritual sanctification begins to emerge in my physical life. It is then I am able to present my body as a living sacrifice and present my members as instruments of righteousness, instead of submitting them to sin (Romans 6:13).

Not one person has fully lived out their sanctification, for we all slip back into the fleshly way of thinking. Even the Apostle Paul acknowledged that he had not yet attained to this; therefore, he was not yet perfected. The inner man cannot sin, for he has been born of God (1 John 3:9), but the outer flesh can. Yet our goal is to walk in our sanctification so our outward behavior can reach toward perfection.

The one who is looking to force their outward behavior into a godly mold by human effort will have a lifetime of failure with moments of perceived success. The one who looks to the Spirit will have a life of success with moments of failure (i.e. slipping back into the flesh).

This is what Paul means by not yet having attained perfection. The life of God is within him through Christ, yet even at the end of his life, he still had to acknowledge he had not reached perfection – that way of living that never fell back into the flesh. Yet even though he said, "Who will deliver me from this body of death," he concluded with the praise, "I thank God through Christ! When I'm in the flesh, I serve the law of sin, but in my mind (on the spirit[37]) I serve the law of God." (Romans 7:24-25) Our new spirit's desire is the same as the Spirit of God, but the flesh seeks its own way.

If you are in Christ, you already have His perfection. Yet when your mind is viewing life through the flesh, His life is not lived through you. In the Spirit, this is a guarantee.

This is yet another reason to stop focusing on sin. It's of the flesh. Once my mind is in the Spirit, sin is no longer my concern. In the flesh, even my good is actually sin. There is no difference between the person who denies Christ's work and tries to replace it with their own righteousness, and the one who denies Christ can satisfy and tries to replace it with lust. There is no difference – except to our fleshly mind. So even when I feel righteous, if I'm not walking by faith, I am still in the flesh. All I can do is focus on what I have been given, walk in it, and leave the fleshly things behind.

When we slip back into the flesh, press ahead toward that high calling and leave the flesh behind again. That is the meaning behind these passages.

This is why Paul can say we have attained, but he has not yet attained. The promise is ours. The victory is an accomplished fact. Yet we can return to the flesh where there is no victory. I know this is a lot to process, but as you meditate on these truths it will become clear that the Christian life is lived by faith and not by human effort. Our role is to not allow ourselves to be drawn back

---

[37] Romans 8:6

into the flesh while reckoning ourselves in the promise. Reckoning is an act of faith. It is to account something as true because of our certainty of God's promise. Let's conclude this chapter with **Romans 6:13-15**

> [13] And do not present your members *as* instruments of unrighteousness to sin, but present yourselves to God as being alive from the dead, and your members *as* instruments of righteousness to God.
> [14] For sin shall not have dominion over you, for you are not under law but under grace.
> [15] What then? Shall we sin because we are not under law but under grace? Certainly not!

Do you believe the promise that sin cannot have dominion over you? Can you submit your body as an instrument of righteousness without first entering the promise? No. We escape sin by trusting in Christ and what He accomplished on the cross. Once we are in the promise, we bring our body under subjection through the Spirit and we then have the power not to submit back under sin.

Notice the difference between what the Bible is teaching and what most Christians believe. We believe we are trying to overcome sin. The Bible teaches that sin has already been overcome through Christ, and we should not submit back under it. Christians believe they must strive for righteousness. The Bible teaches that we are the righteousness of Christ.

Many Christians believe sin overcomes them and they are fighting to defeat the body of sin. The Bible teaches that sin died with our body of sin on the cross. Sin cannot have dominion over us, and it cannot overcome you.

Anyone who is living their Christian life through personal effort is already in sin, for as the Bible says (even to the Christian) the body is dead because of sin, but the Spirit is life because of righteousness. If you try to live the Christian life through the flesh, you are trying to force righteous behavior into a body that can do nothing but serve sin. Yet if you are walking by faith, you can then rule your body from the position of righteousness and learn how to stop falling back into a fleshly way of thinking.

What's more is that when we sin, we have the promise that Jesus is our Advocate, or the one who pleads our innocence. If we believe this, we can step back into faith and leave the body of sin behind. It has no dominion over the person walking by faith.

It's not your work. It's God's. When you reckon God's promises to be true and walk by faith in Christ, God has promised to subdue your iniquities and mature you into righteousness. His Spirit empowers you to walk in His righteousness.

The Christian life is a struggle for one reason – that you may fully understand that the power is in God and not in us.[38] Anything not of faith robs God of His glory. To be of faith is to be focusing on Christ and believing in what He has done and given. Those who walk by faith have the guarantee of victory, for it is God's power that is revealed in the life of those who are trusting fully in Him.

Your sin was crucified with Christ. Your body of sin was crucified with Christ. Your sins and old sinful nature was buried with Christ. You were raised into life so that you can walk in the newness of life. Now reckon yourself to be dead indeed to sin, but alive in Christ. That is when the Christian life truly begins!

---

[38] 2 Corinthians 4:7

The Crucified Life

Discussion Questions

Can the flesh use the concept of grace for itself?

Can God's grace be truly received through the flesh?

Can you think of any other doctrines that unbelievers have used for self-serving purposes? Does this abuse nullify what the Bible is teaching?

Explain what it means to be buried with Christ.

How did Jesus pay for your sins before you were born, i.e. before you committed them?

If Christ already purchased your salvation, why didn't you experience grace before you became a Christian?

Why are Christians defeated, even though the Bible promises they are already overcomers?

Can you will yourself into righteousness?

What is the difference between presenting your body as a tool for righteousness, and trying to use your body to produce righteousness?

Why does God allow Christians to struggle and experience failure?

Is our failure a barrier to God?

Explain what it means to be crucified with Christ.

Reaping and Sowing

We've all heard that we reap what we sow, but my goal is to change the way you look at this concept. Most teaching is based on human reasoning instead of from the perspective of walking in the Spirit. Let's begin by looking at **Galatians 6:7-9**

> 7 Do not be deceived, God is not mocked; for whatever a man sows, that he will also reap.
> 8 For he who sows to his flesh will of the flesh reap corruption, but he who sows to the Spirit will of the Spirit reap everlasting life.
> 9 And let us not grow weary while doing good, for in due season we shall reap if we do not lose heart.

People tend to view this from one of two perspectives, and I believe both common viewpoints miss the heart of what is being said. One perspective is that if we sin, God is going to get us. If you live contrary to the commandments of God, you will reap the wrath of God. This idea can be dispelled with one passage – **Romans 5:8-9**

> 8 But God demonstrates His own love toward us, in that while we were still sinners, Christ died for us.
> 9 Much more then, having now been justified by His blood, we shall be saved from wrath through Him.

While in sin we received God's grace, but as people who are now God's children, we see the promise of 'much more then'. As children, we have a greater expectation through faith. Through Him, Jesus Christ, we have escaped wrath. There is no double-jeopardy with God. Either Jesus paid for your sins and bore the wrath against sin for you, or He did not. If Jesus satisfied the wrath of judgment against sin, then we cannot reap the wrath of God through our sins. If this passage doesn't convince you, meditate on **1 Thessalonians 5:9**

For God did not appoint us to wrath, but to obtain salvation through our Lord Jesus Christ,

If you are in Christ, you are appointed to obtain salvation. Romans tells us we are saved from wrath, and this passage affirms that promise.

The second misconception of sowing and reaping is that if we sow good deeds we'll reap rewards. This is partially true, but misses an important point. We've discussed this previously. Jesus said that many will present their good works to Him, but will be told, "You are a worker of sin." This is in spite of the fact they served in Jesus' name, and did the types of works Jesus said the church should be doing.

The promise of reaping and sowing hinges on one main point – either we are sowing in the flesh, or sowing in the Spirit. Good deeds through human effort are still works of the flesh. This means that any good work must be a work of the Spirit and not accomplished through the flesh.

Many well-meaning people do good deeds outside of obedience to God. Even atheists do things they believe are good. Many atheists have sacrificed their lives for what they believed was right and good. Secular governments are often anti-Christian, but they feed the poor and do many good deeds for people. Yet according to the scriptures, people who do seemingly good deeds can be sowing in the flesh and are still performing acts of lawlessness.

We can sow in the flesh in many ways. The more obvious ways are to steal, kill, lust, pursue greed, hate others, commit adultery, and many other acts of blatant sin. Indeed, those who sow this in their lives will reap the consequences. What's more is that it isn't God that is going to get them in this life. Sin itself produces death through the flesh and all its entrapments. Look at **Romans 6:16**

Do you not know that to whom you present yourselves slaves to obey, you are that one's slaves whom you obey, whether of sin *leading* to death, or of obedience *leading* to righteousness?

Sin itself produces death. Even the Christian can submit back under the slavery of sin. The above passage is written to Christians. Do you not know that if you submit back to sin, you become its slave and can only expect to reap death? The flesh is the way of death. This is not speaking of spiritual death, for the Bible also addresses sinful Christians many times. One man in the church of Corinth was openly living in immorality and was unrepentant. He was turned over to Satan for the destruction of the flesh so that the judgment of sin in this life might lead him to mercy.[39]

When this man turned from his sin, the church was commanded to receive him back into the church, comfort him, and affirm their love toward him.[40] The consequences of sin drove him to the understanding that sin has no worth. He began reaping from the flesh, and he didn't like what his life was receiving. The consequences of reaping leads us to mercy – not damnation. We are not paying for sin; we are reaping the fruit of sin. When sin drives us to brokenness, we find that God is already waiting with the hand of grace.

The Bible tells us that all sin falls into one of three categories. It is either the lust of the eyes, the lust of the flesh, or the pride of life.[41] The lust of the eyes is easy for us to comprehend. That's greed, covetousness, and wanting all the pleasures of life from the world. The lust of the flesh is also easy to spot. It is lust, cravings, and any spiritually unhealthy urge. It's the longing of the flesh to have its desires met through varying types of physical pleasures. While these things are not evil in themselves, when desire is the driving force of our lives, or we believe fulfillment can only come through our cravings, they fall outside of God's design and our lives are drawn into sin.

Either satisfaction is a gift of God, or it is the lust of the flesh. One is receiving by faith from a life focused on Christ, the other is

---

[39] 1 Corinthians 5:5
[40] 2 Corinthians 2:6-8
[41] 1 John 2:16

Reaping and Sowing

a life focused on the flesh as we try to fulfill ourselves. One trusts in God; the other trusts in the object of our desire.

The pride of life is a harder sin to recognize. Pride mimics joy or confidence while putting our focus on self instead of Christ. Because we are human, we'll never be able to be selfless. We can have moments of selfless acts, but ultimately everything we do has a selfish motive behind it. We do good to others because it makes us feel good. We give to receive. We either receive return favors, or we receive self-focused honor.

The greatest form of the pride of life is self-righteousness. From the outside, there is no way we can tell if someone is trusting in Christ's righteousness, or their own. And that is not for us to judge. What is for us to judge is our own focus. To understand this better, let's look at **Romans 7:18**

> For I know that in me (that is, in my flesh) nothing good dwells; for to will is present with me, but *how* to perform what is good I do not find.

Anyone looking at the Apostle Paul's life would have seen a life of sacrifice and giving. Yet Paul looked at himself and lamented that though he desired to do good, he could not find anything within his own flesh that could produce that good. He goes on to mourn of the fact that sin rises up through his flesh, produces unrighteousness, and he does what he knows is wrong, but can't seem to do what he knows is right. He ends his lamentation with both the problem and the solution. Look at **Romans 7:24-25**

> [24] O wretched man that I am! Who will deliver me from this body of death?
> [25] I thank God-- through Jesus Christ our Lord! So then, with the mind I myself serve the law of God, but with the flesh the law of sin.

In the flesh, the Apostle Paul (the one God used to pen two-thirds of the New Testament), lamented that he had no power to do good outside of Christ. When he sowed in the flesh through human effort, instead of finding good, he reaped sin through the flesh. He who sows in the flesh will reap corruption. That is true whether you think you are doing good or are pursuing sin.

Yet immediately after acknowledging the hopelessness of his condition, he rejoices in the solution. This is for you as well! Even when you are in the sorrow of failure, lift your eyes and see. Thank God that even though in the flesh you can do nothing worthy of a reward and cannot find good – true good, in Christ you have the guarantee of victory.

Let's digress for a moment. Before you were born into the Spirit, you had a sinful nature. That nature was ruled by the flesh and could do nothing other than gratify itself. Sometimes it felt gratified by feeling righteous; sometimes it felt gratified by pursuing lust. In reality both are acts of sin, for both lust and self-righteousness are acts of rejection of Christ's work.

When God revealed Himself to you, the Spirit unveiled the joy of salvation, which caused you to recognize the corruption of sin. Sin looked good when it convinced you it had value, but once the value of eternal life came into view, everything else became worthless. By faith, you received Christ, and the Spirit of God performed what the Bible calls 'the circumcision without hands'.[42] The old nature was circumcised out of your heart, buried with Christ, and a new spirit was born, whose life is in Christ. This can be better understood by looking at **Romans 6:6-7**

[6] Knowing this, that our old man was crucified with *Him*,
that the body of sin might be done away with, that we
should no longer be slaves of sin.

[7] For he who has died has been freed from sin.

I'm using the New King James version of the Bible. Many versions translate 'done away with' as 'destroyed'. Many times the Bible says that the body is still under the power of sin, yet this passage seems to indicate that the body of sin is gone. This can be confusing unless we dig behind the translation and look at the original Greek.

---

[42] Colossians 2:11

Reaping and Sowing

The word translated as 'destroyed' or 'done away with' comes from the Greek word 'katargeo', which means: to render idle, inactivated, or unemployed. Depending on the context, it can also be translated as destroyed, abolished, ceased, or other similar words. Yet in this context, it is clear that our body hasn't been destroyed. Not only that, the book of Romans goes on to explain that the body is very much alive and causes us problems.

In Christ the body has been done away with as our ruler. It has been unemployed and dethroned from its previous position of power over us. It is for this reason that the flesh wars against our minds as it attempts to recapture control. It is unemployed; therefore, it must steal control over us in order to employ our minds to do its bidding – to gratify the desires of the flesh.

The body of flesh remains, and sin dwells within the body. This is explained in **Romans 7:20-23**

[20] Now if I do what I will not *to do*, it is no longer I who do it, but sin that dwells in me.

[21] I find then a law, that evil is present with me, the one who wills to do good.

[22] For I delight in the law of God according to the inward man.

[23] But I see another law in my members, warring against the law of my mind, and bringing me into captivity to the law of sin which is in my members.

Notice, sin's origin is not from you, but from the sin that dwells in your members – or flesh. Take note of another important truth here. When your sinful nature was taken away by God, sin was displaced. It no longer has power over you, for the sin nature it ruled is no longer present. You only had one nature then, and you only have one nature now. The old nature was born after the sin of Adam, but the new nature is born of God. As we've already studied, the new nature cannot sin, for it is born of God.

That is why Paul said, "It is no longer I, but sin that dwells in my flesh." The Bible also states, "The body is dead because of sin, but the spirit is life because of righteousness."[43] This is written to the Christian – the one who is a new creation in Christ. Your body is still dead in sin, but sin no longer has an outlet. For this reason, when the body craves sin, it wars against your mind, trying to bring you back into captivity to sin.

Sin cannot operate without first taking over your mind. You must be drawn into the flesh before sin can have control. That's why the Bible tells us that sin has no power. But the Bible also says that we can submit ourselves to sin to obey it in its lusts. It is the working of sin that seeks to rule you and make you into its slave to serve the body of flesh.

Many Christians are under sin's bondage, and they can't find a way of escape because they try to defeat sin by sowing in the flesh. The Bible says that the answer is to submit to the Spirit and reckon (or account) ourselves dead indeed to sin, but most people are taught to get into sin's arena and try to wrestle it under submission.

The body of flesh can never bring sin into submission. Once sin's craving is temporarily satisfied, it may lie dormant for a time, but when it hungers to be gratified, your best efforts are but temporary roadblocks. You will sin in the flesh. As I've stated before, you are already sinning when you try to overcome temptation by human effort. That is still sowing in the flesh, and attempting to become righteous by personal effort is to make oneself a rival to the righteousness of Christ. And God has no rivals.

The solution is not to try harder. Nor is it to grovel in guilt and failure. If you try to overcome, you will discover the lamentation of the Apostle Paul and cry out, "Who will deliver me from this body of sin and death?" Hopefully you will discover the same answer he found, "I thank God through Christ Jesus."

The answer is not in your efforts or resistance. With the flesh you can do nothing but serve the law of sin. With the mind in the Spirit, you can do nothing but serve the law of God. Both are natural acts. The flesh will serve what it craves. Your new nature will serve what it craves. One is empowered when we operate

---

[43] Romans 8:10

through the flesh, the other is empowered when we operate out of faith.

Faith is trusting in God. Just as the Bible says, "Abraham believed God, and his faith was accounted to him for righteousness," the same is true for you. Your righteousness comes only as God's gift when you trust Him and take Him at His word. If you don't believe His promise will work, keep trying to do it through human effort. Of course you will also keep reaping through the flesh.

Your victory is God's work. Your role is to trust in Him. The human intellect looks at sin and says, "How can just believing defeat sin?" It can't. It is God who defeats sin. When we trust Him, the Holy Spirit performs the work of purifying our minds and subduing the flesh. Either you are in control, or the Spirit is in control. There can't be two masters. He sets you free from sin and the flesh so you can walk in the Spirit without distraction. God doesn't want you to clean up the flesh. God wants you to believe Him and walk by faith. Take to heart the words of **1 Corinthians 1:18**

> For the message of the cross is foolishness to those who are perishing, but to us who are being saved it is the power of God.

To the carnal mind, this message is foolish. Even a Christian, if he or she is drawing from the same human understanding that the perishing world trusts in, will say this message is foolish. I've been called foolish by many well-meaning Christians who believe that ceasing from human effort will empower sin. Yet the message of the cross is that human effort *is* empowering sin, and the one who walks by faith is outside of sin's grasp. Meditate on **Galatians 5:18**

> But if you are led by the Spirit, you are not under the law.

Throughout the New Testament we are told that the believer is no longer under the law. The law has come to an end in Christ. Now we see that if you are led by the Spirit, you are not under the law. Why? Because our inner man delights in the law of God and needs no outside requirement to drive him away from sin.

The Christian walking by faith needs no law. Let's let the Bible explain why this is true. Look at **Romans 2:14-15a**

14 for when Gentiles, who do not have the law, by nature do the things in the law, these, although not having the law, are a law to themselves,

15 who show the work of the law written in their hearts,

This was written to the Jewish Christian in the era of the Apostle Paul. A Gentile is anyone who is not of Jewish descent. The Jewish people who were looking to the law were missing the message of Christ. To help Jewish Christians coming out of the law system understand the New Covenant, the Bible points to the Gentiles as the example of God's work.

These people didn't know the law, were not raised under the law, and did not have a clue about the law or religious traditions. Yet something within them caused them to act according to God's ways without having any rules to direct them. This proved that God had written the law on their hearts through the new nature they were born into.

This is why Paul said, "I delight in the law of God according to the inner man." Our new nature is of God, in God, and by God. Its nature is born of God; therefore, our inner man desires the same things God desires. It is only when our minds are submitted to the flesh that we stop acting according to who we are. Then instead of turning back to faith, religion teaches us to employ new rules (laws) in an attempt to curb the flesh and force it back into an acceptable standard.

Under this form of Christianized religion, the best they can hope for is a pretense of righteousness, for they are trusting in legalism instead of learning how to walk according to their new nature.

If you sow (or invest) your life in the flesh – whether that be religious flesh or openly sinful flesh – you will reap from the flesh.

If you sow in the Spirit by walking by faith and renewing your mind so it is no longer on carnal things, you will reap righteousness and life. The inner man can do nothing other than walk in righteousness. Only when our minds are submitted to the flesh do we begin to see our lives reaping from the flesh.

To the natural mind, the way of faith is foolishness. Don't let carnally minded Christians persuade you to keep sowing in the flesh. Don't let people poison your minds by persuading you that faith in Christ alone will cause you to sin. Trusting in grace cannot produce sin, for if you sow in the Spirit, God's promise is that you will reap from the Spirit. The Spirit cannot produce sin.

Trust God. Sow in faith and reap in joy!

Discussion Questions

Read Romans 5:8-9. Explain why God says we are much more justified than those who are just receiving salvation.

Can we sow in the flesh even if we are laboring for Jesus? Explain.

Is it possible for us to know if someone's works are based on self-righteousness or Christ's righteousness?

Are these warnings of scripture given for us to evaluate the motives of others, or to examine ourselves?

Read Romans 7:20-23. Why does the Bible say that when the Christian sins, it is no longer 'I', but sin that dwells in the person?

How can we have an incorruptible nature and still have sin dwelling in us?

How does our flesh become empowered to sin?

Can the flesh force us to sin against our will?

How do we become fleshly minded?

Why did new Gentile believers suddenly act like righteous people without rules?

Why do new believers seem immune to sin at first, but then start slipping back into sin after a few months?

How do we overcome sin?

The Act of Abiding

Let's begin this chapter with a section of Jesus' final teachings to the disciples before He was crucified. In the Gospel of John from chapter 13 through 17, we find some of the richest truths in the Bible. Jesus packs His final teaching with many things. It's one of my favorite sections of the Bible.

We are jumping into the middle of His teaching, and to do justice to the complete thought of Jesus' teaching on abiding, there aren't any passages we can skip over and still capture the depth of what he is saying. Take a few minutes to soak in His explanation of abiding in Him found in **John 15:3-11**

³ "You are already clean because of the word which I have spoken to you.

⁴ "Abide in Me, and I in you. As the branch cannot bear fruit of itself, unless it abides in the vine, neither can you, unless you abide in Me.

⁵ "I am the vine, you *are* the branches. He who abides in Me, and I in him, bears much fruit; for without Me you can do nothing.

⁶ "If anyone does not abide in Me, he is cast out as a branch and is withered; and they gather them and throw *them* into the fire, and they are burned.

⁷ "If you abide in Me, and My words abide in you, you will ask what you desire, and it shall be done for you.

⁸ "By this My Father is glorified, that you bear much fruit; so you will be My disciples.

⁹ "As the Father loved Me, I also have loved you; abide in My love.

¹⁰ "If you keep My commandments, you will abide in My love, just as I have kept My Father's commandments and abide in His love.

¹¹ "These things I have spoken to you, that My joy may remain in you, and *that* your joy may be full.

This passage begins with Jesus' statement, "You are already clean because of the word I have spoken to you." This is the position of every Christian. God has declared you clean, and from that position of righteousness, we begin walking in the Spirit by faith. We believe in God's word. Let's add another passage to help bring the reality of our spiritual condition into focus. Look at **John 12:46**

> I have come *as* a light into the world, that whoever believes in Me should not abide in darkness.

What makes us clean? It is by God's declaration through His word. How do we escape darkness? By believing in Jesus Christ – who is the word made flesh.[44] Faith comes by hearing the word of God,[45] and once we receive that faith and trust in Him, we are made clean and escape the darkness of sin. From the reality of that position through Christ, we begin the walk of faith by abiding in Him.

The message is to abide – not become. You are not trying to make yourself clean; you are already clean when you put your trust in God's word of truth. The person trying to become righteous or trying to make themselves clean is not walking by faith. The person trying to eradicate sin from their own life is not trusting in the power of God.

I realize I'm throwing a lot of scriptures at the reader, but it's important to see how the entire New Testament is pointing you to the same main point. You are clean, not because of what you do. Not because of what you don't do. You are clean because you have been cleansed. What's more, the daily struggle of sin is driven out, not by human effort, but by turning from your self-efforts and receiving of God. God drives sin out of your life. You cannot make yourself pure *for* Him. He makes you pure *for* Himself. And as you receive of Him, sin and all the works of the flesh are driven out. To help understand this truth, let's bring in **2 Peter 1:3-4**

---

[44] John 1:1, 14
[45] Romans 10:17

The Act of Abiding

³ His divine power has given to us all things that *pertain* to life and godliness, through the knowledge of Him who called us by glory and virtue,

⁴ by which have been given to us exceedingly great and precious promises, that through these you may be partakers of the divine nature, having escaped the corruption *that is* in the world through lust.

Where does our righteousness and goodness come from? His divine power has imparted these into you.

How do you escape the lusts of the world? You receive of God. His divine power cleanses you, and as you partake of Him, lust has no place. Sin will be driven out of your life as you are filled with the power of God's Spirit. And all you have to do is believe and receive of Him.

As a partaker of God's own nature, you have the promise that you receive from Him these things to add to what you already have been given – faith. Add to your faith virtue, knowledge, self-control, perseverance, godliness, brotherly kindness, love (agape). These are not a list of things to accomplish. This is the fruit of the Spirit, given to you as you abide in Christ.

Spiritual growth is the process of learning how to trust in His divine power, receive of God's divine nature, and as your life is filled with the Spirit, the flesh is driven more and more out of your life. Not only are you given the promise of the fruit of the Spirit – which is maturing in the Spirit – but you are also promised that you will have a fruitful life. Reread the passage above from John 15. These passages are speaking of the same things.

You cannot bear fruit unless you abide in Christ. If you abide in Christ, bearing fruit is a guarantee. It's not something you must do or accomplish, it is the natural flow of God through you. The end of the promise is that God is glorified when you blossom and bear fruit. This ties right into **2 Peter 1:8**

For if these things are yours and abound, *you* will be neither barren nor unfruitful in the knowledge of our Lord Jesus Christ.

You cannot be unfruitful if the fruit of the Spirit is abounding in your life. Your soul cannot be barren. You cannot fail. If you continue reading down to 2 Peter 1:10, God gives this promise, "For if you do these things, you will never stumble."

Never stumble? Do you stumble in your Christian walk? We all do, but as the fruit of the Spirit grows in us, the things that cause us to stumble are forced out. They have no place.

What are the 'things we must do'? Some people read this and say, "It says if you do these things; therefore, we must produce virtue, godliness, love, self-control, and all the commands of this passage."

Is this true? I was taught this is a list of commands we must bring about in our own lives. I was taught that God promises fruit if I accomplish these things. But this misses the plainly stated truth of this passage. It begins with the promise, "His divine power has given us all things that pertain to life and godliness."

Everything I need for life has already been given to me through Christ. Everything I need to live a life of godliness has been given to me through Christ. All things means all things.

So what is the 'do' when the Bible says, "If you do these things you will never stumble?" The do is to trust. When the people came to Jesus and said, "What must we do to do the works of God?" Jesus said, "This is the work of God, that you believe on Him (Christ) whom the Father has sent."[46]

This is the 'do' for you as well. The do is to believe the promise, and through your abiding relationship with God, you receive from His nature and add these things to your life. The do is to put your complete trust in Him. Then as you abide in Christ and His word abides in you, it can do nothing but bear fruit. This is the promise.

Most Christians approach spiritual life as though they must accomplish two things. First, they must remove the sinful behaviors that are barriers between themselves and God. If they manage to have a moment of success, then they must do some type of good

---

[46] John 6:28-29

The Act of Abiding

work that pleases God. We are bringing our offering to God in the hopes He will accept us. As long as we accomplish these two things, we feel accepted by God.

If you live the Christian life this way, you will never experience victory. You will always be trying to placate an angry God, and you will always be wondering how much sacrifice is enough. Then the next time you fail in either area, you will lose confidence in His love and the perpetual cycle will begin again. What's worse is that both of these efforts are idols in the Christian's heart. They are not honoring God. These are attempts to raise ourselves up in honor hoping we can measure up to God. Both of these acts of human effort displease God – even if we manage to please ourselves.

The only acceptable sacrifice was Christ, and His sacrifice is given to you as a free gift. As for your sin, the Bible says that it also has been taken out of the way.[47] Both methods of attempting to placate God are actually denying Christ. And the Bible says that if we deny Him, He will deny us. Or as **Titus 1:16** puts it:

> They profess to know God, but in works they deny *Him,* being abominable, disobedient, and disqualified for every good work.

Are your works denying Christ? This passage is not talking about people who were neglecting God and pursuing the world. This is speaking about people who professed God, but attempted to make themselves righteous with good works by human effort. They denied Christ by trying to accomplish in themselves the works Jesus had already accomplished and offered to them by faith. They were trying to accomplish what Jesus had already done; therefore, their attempt of good works were denying the truth of what Christ had already done.

I won't go into the completed work of Christ here since the book, *It is Finished,* and *Abounding Grace,* go into this topic in greater detail.

Your role is not to do God's works, but to abide in God's works. What's more is that Jesus commanded that we abide in His

---

[47] Colossians 2:14

love. Grace is the love of God given to us, and by faith we receive and abide in that love.

You already have the love of God. If you are born in the Spirit by receiving Christ, you are already in the love of God. The command is to abide, not to obtain. In fact, you are not even commanded to love God.

Now that is a shocker for most people. The Old Testament's underlying command was to love God. As we examined earlier, it was to reveal to man that his love is insufficient. The law said, "Do you love God with all your heart, mind, soul, and strength (all, not most)." Anyone who fell short of the command to love with ALL your being was proven to be guilty of all the law.

The underlying principle of the New Testament is God's love for us. Or as the Bible explains in **1 John 4:10**

In this is love, not that we loved God, but that He loved us and sent His Son *to be* the propitiation for our sins.

Is this the message you've been hearing in church? Not that you love God, but that He loves you? If your church background is like mine, you've probably been beaten up with the criticism that you don't love God enough. But since man cannot produce agape love, it is impossible to fulfill the command to love God through your human emotions.

It's not about your love for God, but God's love for you. The failure of the law of the Old Testament is the weakness of the flesh. Your flesh. My flesh. The Old Testament saint's flesh. The law which said, "If you fail to love God or offend the law on any point, you are guilty of all," was taken out of the way when Jesus became our propitiation. Propitiation means that one person stands in the place of judgment for someone else.

God knew man was incapable of agape love. The law was given to reveal this to man so we could understand what love truly is. Then God unveiled His love through Christ and said, "It's not about your love for Me, but My love for you."

Is there any greater revelation? This *is* the gospel! This is the good news!

Now the command is to abide in God's love. By faith we enter into that love, and each command in the New Testament is designed to keep us in His love, teach us how to reveal His love to others, and point us in the direction where we can experience new depths of His love.

The average person looks at God's commands as, "If I do these things, God will receive me." God presents His commands this way, "You have My love. You are already clean, justified, and set apart as an heir of the kingdom. Now obey these commands so you are not drawn away from what I have given you."

Do you see the difference between the law and grace? One is trying to obtain the impossible. The other is God accomplishing the impossible and showing us how to abide in what He has already accomplished for us.

If you abide you will bear fruit. That's because a healthy branch already has what it needs to flourish. It doesn't need to gain anything. All it must do is abide in what it has. Only when it is detached from the vine does it wither and fail to produce fruit. Now the command is to abide. You already have God's complete acceptance and He has given you all things that pertain to life and godliness. You only need to abide in Him by faith as you also learn how to receive the gifts of the Spirit and allow His work to bear fruit in your life.

If you are in Christ, you are already where you need to be. Abide. Don't allow life to draw you away. Don't allow guilt and feelings of condemnation to draw you away. Receive His love, allow it to drive the things of the flesh out of your life, and leave God to deal with your weaknesses. And you have the promise that God's strength is perfected in your weakness. As the Apostle Paul said, "I will glory in my weaknesses and infirmities that the power of God may rest upon me."

This is not only your inability to accomplish good, but it also applies to your tendency to fall into sin. Stop trying to strengthen your weaknesses, but rejoice in them. You are not rejoicing in the sin, but are rejoicing in the weakness that causes you to sin, for that is when you look to Him and experience His power to subdue sin.

When you rejoice in your weakness, He becomes your strength. Your weaknesses are the opportunities to experience the fullness of God. That is when you stop focusing on yourself, and begin looking to Him through faith.

God doesn't want you to eradicate sin. God wants you to trust in Him. Your sin is not His barrier. Your sin is the opportunity for grace to abound and the power of God to overcome what you could never control.

One of the command we read in 2 Peter is for you to add self-control to your life. This is of the fruit of the Spirit, not the accomplishment of your ability to change yourself. Not only does God promise to deliver us from our transgressions,[48] but look at the promise of **Psalm 34:22**

The LORD redeems the soul of His servants, And none of those who trust in Him shall be condemned.

The Lord wants you to trust in Him. The condemnation is not to those who sin, but to those who never learn to trust in God's redemption. The flesh can do nothing but sin. The one who walks by faith will experience righteousness, and the works of the flesh will be displaced by the fruit of the Spirit!

---

[48] Psalm 39:8

The Act of Abiding

Discussion Questions

According to Jesus, what makes us clean?

Read 2 Peter 1:3-8. According to this passage, how are these spiritual attributes received into our lives?

Do we produce these spiritual things for God? Explain.

Read John 15:4-5. According to this passage and 2 Peter 1, how does the Christian become fruitful?

God promised that He has given us all things that pertain to life and godliness. What does this exclude?

What is the thing we must do as mentioned in 2 Peter 1:10?

When does good works become an idol?

Review 1 John 4:10 and Deuteronomy 6:5. How does the concept of love differ under the Old Covenant and the New Covenant?

Read Romans 8:3-4. How does the Old Testament Law reveal the love of God in the New Testament?

Does God expect you to eradicate sin from your life? Explain.

Is sin a barrier to God? Why or why not?

Is glorying in your weaknesses an acceptance of sin?

Where Sin Dwells

Let's begin this chapter by looking at **Romans 7:18**

> For I know that in me (that is, in my flesh) nothing good dwells; for to will is present with me, but *how* to perform what is good I do not find.

As stated previously, most people try to serve God through their flesh. By flesh I mean by human effort – it's our natural ability trying to accomplish something spiritual. Jesus said, "What is born of the flesh is flesh. That which is born of the Spirit is spirit."[49]

This basic truth is hard for Christians to grasp. We want to believe we can produce good. From the human perspective, man's goodness looks good. But consider the life of the Apostle Paul. He spent his entire life learning the scriptures, living by the highest standard of perfection man could achieve, and yet when he encountered Christ, Paul said, "I count it all as trash."

The book of Romans was written to explain this very thing to the Christians coming out of the Jewish mindset of the Old Testament. Using his experience as an example, Paul said that even though his desire is to do good, when he looks to himself he cannot find any good by which he may perform the works of God.

The reason Paul understood this truth is because he fully understood this battle between the flesh and the Spirit. The flesh can do many deeds that appear good, but every deed is still of the flesh. The flesh doesn't sacrifice; it invests. It gives in order to receive. The one thing the flesh craves the most is honor. We want people to look at us and say, "What a good person."

It is impossible for you to be completely selfless. It is impossible for you to produce good. It is impossible for you to do anything acceptable to God without God's Spirit bearing fruit through you. Take to heart the words of **James 1:17-18**

---

[49] John 3:6

82   Where Sin Dwells

^{17} Every good gift and every perfect gift is from above, and comes down from the Father of lights, with whom there is no variation or shadow of turning.
^{18} Of His own will He brought us forth by the word of truth, that we might be a kind of firstfruits of His creatures.

Everything that is good must first come from above. By good, I mean good from the eternal perspective. Even an ungodly man can perform random acts of kindness and do things that appear good. Yet these are still of the flesh. Good is the fruit of the Spirit, not the works of man, or as **1 Corinthians 15:10b** puts it:
I labored more abundantly than they all, yet not I, but the grace of God *which was* with me.

Until you understand you can do nothing but produce sin, you will keep laboring by human effort and producing works of the flesh. Like counterfeits, it may look good on the surface, but when examined against the real thing it is shown to be worthless.

Now let's look at the flesh from the perspective of the Spirit. Just as our good deeds appear to us as reward-worthy but are not, our sins that appear to be punishment worthy, are nullified in the Spirit. Good deeds accomplished through the flesh being counted as worthless seems like bad news, but knowing our bad deeds are counted as meaningless is good news indeed!

Once you grasp this fundamental truth, it will transform your life. However, it's hard to get people to understand this because the moment the discussion begins, most jump to a conclusion based on how the flesh would live if it had the same freedom. The fleshly mind that is focused on religion will reject this important principle, not knowing that this will free them from self-created guilt and self-condemnation.

On the other hand, the fleshly mind that is focused on the indulgence of the flesh will embrace the carnal concept of grace, and seek to exploit God's promises for fleshly purposes. Both the religious and the indulgent mind on the flesh are in the same boat. They sit at opposite ends of the boat, thinking they are not in the flesh, but outside of the Spirit, the fruit of the flesh is the flesh. This is true whether the carnal mind is masquerading as religious piety or masquerading as religious freedom. God's Spirit works through the Spirit, and anyone not in the Spirit will reject or exploit God's word, but both remain outside the promise.

As discussed earlier, anything in the flesh is sin. We want to say that sin is lusting after someone, committing acts of sexual immorality, stealing, violence, and other 'big' sins. What most fail to grasp is that they are already guilty of these sins and more. In the flesh, your condition is absolutely hopeless. To bring the reality of this into focus, let's review the Bible's examples of sin.

- It's a sin to stop praying for someone – even if they have rejected God. 1 Samuel 12:23
- Rebellion is equal to witchcraft – 1 Samuel 15:23
- Our stubbornness is equal to idolatry – 1 Samuel 15:23
- To know good and not do it is sin – James 4:17
- To have lust in your heart is adultery – Matthew 5:28
- To have anger in your heart is sin – Matthew 5:22
- To call someone worthless is sin – Matthew 5:22
- To call someone an idiot puts us in danger of hell fire – Matthew 5:22
- The person who hates in their heart is a murderer – 1 John 3:15
- Pursuing passions, evil desires, or to want something you don't have is idolatry – Colossians 3:5
- Wicked imaginations is a sin – Proverbs 6:18
- To even have a proud look is a sin – Proverbs 6:17
- To fail to love God or love your neighbor in any way breaks all the commandments – Matthew 22:37-40
- Any thought or action on our part, or to even eat without faith in God is sin – Romans 14:23

Finally, let's look at the passage that drives home our absolutely desperate need of God's grace, **James 2:10**

For whoever shall keep the whole law, and yet stumble in one *point*, he is guilty of all.

Do you see why it's a complete misunderstanding of our helpless condition to believe we can be right with God based on what we do or don't do? Do you see that if you are in the flesh, you are guilty of the whole law, for the flesh cannot measure up to God's standard of perfection? Not only that, but the flesh can do nothing but sin.

The sin nature was removed by the circumcision of Christ,[50] and now the body of flesh is dethroned.[51] It has no sinful nature it can employ to serve its desires; therefore, it seeks to war against our minds to bring us back into captivity to sin.[52] The sin is in charge when you are in the flesh. This is true – even if you think you are doing good.

The good news is that sin and the flesh have no power over you. Once you understand the difference between your life in the Spirit and the mind in the flesh, you can begin learning how to trust in God's grace and walk by faith. What's even better is you will also begin understanding how irrelevant sin is in the Christian's life.

Before understanding your life in the Spirit, you thought you were living righteously if you didn't do the blatant sins. If you understand that in your flesh nothing is good, then you also understand that your attempts of righteous deeds are just as much acts of rebellion against the Spirit as your evil desires.

And here is the good news. It doesn't matter – if you walk in the Spirit. If you have only been taught the 'behave yourself and God is pleased' gospel, this may seem strange to you. So let's dig a little deeper. Look at **Romans 3:19**

> Now we know that whatever the law says, it says to those who are under the law, that every mouth may be stopped, and all the world may become guilty before God.

Who is the focus of this condemnation? The law proclaims the guilt of those who are under the law. Anyone not under the law

---

[50] Colossians 2:11
[51] Romans 6:6
[52] Romans 7:23

cannot be found guilty, for the law does not apply. I am about to bring in a lot of scriptures. In fact, there are so many passages that teach on this very topic, I'm amazed the church does not understand this. I spent the first few decades of my Christian life trying to satisfy God's requirements and being ignorant of this clear teaching of scripture. Not only is the church ignorant of this truth, but people fight against it when it is taught because it undermines their claims of righteousness.

The church's failure to believe in God's righteousness is the same as the world's failure to believe in Christ's salvation. It seems foolish until someone experiences its reality. The Christian life is lived the same way it is entered – by faith in Christ alone.

Don't' shut down the word of God when it goes outside of your comfort zone or church traditions.

As we have just read, the law was intended to proclaim the guilt to those who are under the law. This is every person who has ever lived, but it stops when a person dies. I'll explain this in a moment, but first look at **Galatians 5:18**

But if you are led by the Spirit, you are not under the law.

Can this truth be denied? The Bible clearly says that if you are being led by the Spirit, you are NOT under the law. According to Romans 8:9, if Christ is in you, you are in the Spirit. The law does not apply to those who are in Christ. The flesh is still bound by the law, and you can submit back under it through both blatant sins and sins of false righteousness, but it has no power – other than your submission to it.

If this is new to you, you might be asking yourself if this is a license to sin. If we are no longer under the law, does that mean we can act any way we want? Do you realize the Apostles of Christ were asked this exact same thing? If the law is not counted against me, does that mean I can sin freely?

Nine times in the book of Romans the Apostle Paul answered this very objection. My favorite of his answers is, "Certainly not! How can we who have died to sin continue to live in it?"[53] Just think

---

[53] Romans 6:2

about this for a moment. Sin and death reigned. It produced death, put us under bondage, heaped guilt and condemnation upon us, and left us with a lifeless spirit. Now we have found life in Christ where the law no longer has power, and people are saying, "If the law has no power, you are just going to use that as an excuse to sin."

How can that not be an absurd statement? I was covered with the stench of death, I was raised from the corpses and given life, and people say that my new Spirit-filled life will only cause me to go back and wallow among the corpses? That doesn't remotely make sense – unless you can only see life from the perspective of death. Let's continue to see how the Bible paints this beautiful picture of life through dying. Look at **Romans 7:4-6**

> 4 Therefore, my brethren, you also have become dead to the law through the body of Christ, that you may be married to another-- to Him who was raised from the dead, that we should bear fruit to God.
> 5 For when we were in the flesh, the sinful passions which were aroused by the law were at work in our members to bear fruit to death.
> 6 But now we have been delivered from the law, having died to what we were held by, so that we should serve in the newness of the Spirit and not *in* the oldness of the letter.

The oldness of the letter is the letter of the law. The Bible calls the law the ministry of death,[54] referring to the fact that the law proclaimed our failures as sin, and the wages of sin is death.

I once had a person rebuke me saying, "The law never passed away, for Jesus said that even if heaven and earth should pass away, My words will never pass away." Yet the Bible says the law that was passing away was glorious, how much more is the ministry of the Spirit more glorious?[55] Is that a contradiction? No.

---

[54] 2 Corinthians 3:7
[55] 2 Corinthians 3:7-8

The law is just as active today as it was in the Old Testament, but only to those who are still in the flesh. This passage helps to explain, **Romans 10:4**

> For Christ *is* the end of the law for righteousness to everyone who believes.

Do you believe God's word? If so, the law has come to an end for everyone who believes in Christ. Let's continue pulling in the pieces of this wonderful promise. Look now at **2 Corinthians 5:17-18**

> [17] Therefore, if anyone *is* in Christ, *he is* a new creation; old things have passed away; behold, all things have become new.
> [18] Now all things *are* of God, who has reconciled us to Himself through Jesus Christ, and has given us the ministry of reconciliation,

As we looked at in a previous chapter, we died with Christ and were raised as a new creation. When we died, old things passed away. Our life in the flesh passed away and is in the grave. Now all things have become new and you have been fully reconciled to God. Do you believe God's word?

You don't have to get rid of your old sins. They were removed in Christ. You don't have to fear judgment, the life under condemnation died. You don't have to try to make your flesh conform to a godly standard. It is still awaiting its final redemption. Until you are changed into His likeness at the resurrection, the flesh cannot be redeemed and is incapable of conforming to a righteous standard. It is incapable of producing righteousness. It is incapable of doing the will of God.

This is why everything is a gift. The Bible says that you become the righteousness of God in Christ. It is a gift. Your righteousness is the righteousness of God. Anything other than God's righteousness gifted to you is a counterfeit work of the flesh. You are holy because you are in Him. To try to make yourself holy by human effort will be rejected. There is nothing you can be, do, or offer to God that

He will accept other than that which He has first given to you. Even your faith is first given to you from God.[56]

Take a few moments to read Romans 8:2-4. We are told that the law of the Spirit of life in Christ has made us free from the law of sin. You are free from that law. I'll ask you again, do you believe God's word? The Bible goes on to explain that the law failed because it depended upon the weakness of the flesh – the same flesh that continues to try to draw us back into sin today.

Since the flesh rendered us incapable of fulfilling the law, Christ came in the flesh and condemned sin in His body of flesh. What we could not do, Jesus accomplished for us, fulfilled the law, and now we who are in Christ are fulfillers of the law simply because we are in Him. We are accounted as righteous by faith in Him alone.

When we believe, we are then promised that the righteous requirement of the law is fulfilled in us for no other reason than the fact we are in the Spirit through faith in Christ. You do not have to accomplish obedience; you have to trust in Christ who was obedient in all things and credits you with His righteousness. Obedience is believing upon Him and abiding in what He has given.

Armed with this understanding, let's now answer the burning question everyone is probably thinking – what about sin in the Christian's life? Does it matter?

Yes, and no. How's that for a clear answer? In reality, the question itself is flawed. The real question is, "Are we going to walk in the flesh where sin dwells, or are we going to walk in the Spirit where righteousness is already alive?"

The reason we examined the plethora of sins identified in the Bible is so you might realize that you are always in sin if you are in the flesh. One man heard this message and said, "You are just trying to find justification for your sin."

Since he knows nothing about my life, I'm not sure which sin he was referring to. Was it when I acted selfishly? Or does he realize that each time I try to become righteous instead of trusting in the righteousness of God, I am in the flesh, where sin reigns?

---

[56] Romans 12:3

Certainly there are people who try to twist grace into an excuse for sin, but how can we use the example of someone living for the flesh as a reason to reject the promise of freedom to walk in the Spirit? And this is the underlying principle – we have been set free.

In the Old Covenant, sin was what bound people to condemnation. They could not come before God's throne because they were bound by the flesh. When Christ died, the veil between the people and the holiest place of God was torn from top to bottom, making it open and accessible to every person. In the Old Covenant, the High Priest had to atone for his sin, go through many cleansing rituals, and they would even tie a rope on his leg in case he failed to obey completely and was struck down for his sin while in the holiest place. Any failure to atone for sin or fail to fulfill the law perfectly was a death sentence. The holiest place in the temple was a fearful place.

In the New Covenant, God has invited us into the holiest place, and now the command is to be confident before Him. We are told to come before God's throne with boldness, knowing we will receive grace for help in our time of need. In our time of need – not when we are worthy enough to come before Him.

We are boldly triumphing over sin, and confidently going to the place where only the High Priest could go once a year. And for him it was a place of dread. For us, it's the place of grace – God's favor. We are bold for one reason – we are in Christ.

The Old Covenant commanded that no one come before the throne without fulfilling all the law's demands. The New covenant COMMANDS us to come before the throne with confidence. We need not fear judgment for our sins, for we are entering through Christ, where all sin has been atoned for and taken out of the way.

When you sin, come before God with confidence. Then the flesh has no power to keep you in bondage. Sin has no power over you, and sin has no right to come with you to the throne of God. You are free to pursue life in the Spirit without the burden of the flesh. God has already taken care of the flesh, and the one who walks by faith has the promise that the flesh and the sin within it has no power.

Though people will accuse the one who walks by faith of excusing sin, the truth is that this is the only Christian who is fully escaping sin. Let's begin wrapping this chapter up by looking at **Romans 7:18-25**

> [18] For I know that in me (that is, in my flesh) nothing good dwells; for to will is present with me, but *how* to perform what is good I do not find.
>
> [19] For the good that I will *to do*, I do not do; but the evil I will not *to do*, that I practice.
>
> [20] Now if I do what I will not *to do*, it is no longer I who do it, but sin that dwells in me.
>
> [21] I find then a law, that evil is present with me, the one who wills to do good.
>
> [22] For I delight in the law of God according to the inward man.
>
> [23] But I see another law in my members, warring against the law of my mind, and bringing me into captivity to the law of sin which is in my members.
>
> [24] O wretched man that I am! Who will deliver me from this body of death?
>
> [25] I thank God-- through Jesus Christ our Lord! So then, with the mind I myself serve the law of God, but with the flesh the law of sin.

I want to point you to some important truths in this passage. First notice that the Apostle Paul, the one God used to pen two-thirds of the New Testament, stated, "How to perform good, I don't find." Why? Because, "In my flesh, nothing good dwells."

This means that even if he could do good by human standards, it still is not good because the flesh is incapable of righteousness.

It's important for you to realize that in your flesh nothing good dwells. Not only does nothing good dwell, but sin and evil do dwell in the flesh. When the Apostle Paul was in the flesh, he could do nothing but serve the law of sin. In the Spirit, he could do nothing but serve the law of God.

The same is true for you. If you are trying to serve God through human effort, you are serving the law of sin. You can expect to produce nothing but the dead works of the flesh, even though it may be labeled with religious names.

Do you see why the earlier question about whether it's okay to sin is flawed? What those who condemn grace-believers don't understand is that their own best and most glossed up efforts and works are nothing but acts of sin produced by the flesh. What they also don't realize is that those who stop trying to do the works of God themselves are the only ones who can ever see the grace of God working through them.

God does enter the works of our own efforts at times and performs His grace in spite of our flesh. If He did not, the church would be in worse shape than it is already in. Yet our works are often the hindrance against God's work because it centers around us instead of resting in the power of Christ.

The average Christian toils through life trying to contain the flesh and only sees moments of God slip through. The one who truly walks by faith begins to see the power of the Spirit become the norm and only moments of the flesh slip through.

When the flesh persuades you to submit, sin emerges, but according to the Bible, "It is not I, but sin that dwells in my members," or body of flesh. Your sins are not you. Your sins only reveal whether your mind is in the flesh or in the Spirit. As Paul stated, with my flesh I serve sin, but with my mind (the mind in the Spirit) I serve the law of God. And you are not keeping the law, but it is your new nature, the person you truly are, that has the natural desires that are in agreement with God. You don't need a law because it is in your nature to walk in righteousness.

The only law you need is the law of faith,[57] for the only effort on our part is to keep our focus on trusting in Christ and not ourselves, our religion, or our methods.

---

[57] Romans 3:27

Perhaps you are experiencing what the Apostle Paul worked through. You desire to do good. That is your new nature. It desires to obey God, walk in righteousness, and enjoy fellowship with your heavenly Father. It is the central part of you. But sin in your flesh desires to be served through the body. It has no nature to employ to do its bidding, so it wars against your mind, seeking to bring you back into captivity to serve sin. You wrestle but can't find the good in your flesh and freedom seems hopeless. Your heart may cry out as the Apostle Paul did, "O wretched man/woman that I am. Who will rescue me from this body of death?"

Notice, the body is where sin dwells. And God is your rescuer. I pray you will find the victory that Paul stated in the very next passage, "I thank God through Jesus Christ!" That is your victory – His power in you. You cannot bring your flesh into a righteous standard – at least not for long. You must be rescued by Christ and brought into the life of the Spirit, where the flesh has no power.

This is why the Bible says, "This is the victory that overcomes the world, our faith." Our flesh is of this world, and our faith in Christ is how we receive His victory. It is all of Him, by Him, and through Him. It is not you becoming right for God. It is about you receiving the righteousness of God through Christ.

Immediately after Paul laments over the fact that his flesh wars against his mind and sometimes brings him back into captivity, he then rejoices in two things. First that he found victory in Christ, and then the chapter breaks, but it is still a continuation of His explanation. Look at **Romans 8:1-2**

> [1] *There is* therefore now no condemnation to those who are in Christ Jesus, who do not walk according to the flesh, but according to the Spirit.
> [2] For the law of the Spirit of life in Christ Jesus has made me free from the law of sin and death.

Even if you fall into sin, there is no condemnation to those who are in Christ! Certainly we don't want to live in the flesh where the law empowers sin. If we abide in the flesh, we'll reap things of the flesh. Things that have no value at best and cause us pain and grief at worst. But sin cannot overcome the work of Christ and any who are in Christ cannot be condemned.

The Bible speaks about the consequences of sin, how the Lord will chastise us to bring us back, and many other things outside the scope of this book. But be aware that you cannot defeat sin. You cannot overcome the flesh. You cannot produce righteousness or good works. Many people are deceived into believing that they can produce righteousness by human effort. Many more are deceived into believing that they can root sin out of their own lives. Others still are duped into believing that sin can defeat them. It's all about faith in Christ.

Either you are walking in faith or you are walking in defeat.

Never lose sight of this important truth. You are the righteousness of God in Christ. You have escaped the law. When sin manages to get a temporary victory, don't sweat the small stuff. Sin has been defeated in your life. It remains in the unredeemed flesh, and when you recognize it in your life, stop groveling and start walking by faith. Guilt is the accusation of the enemy, but the Bible says that if we sin, we have an Advocate with the Father, Jesus Christ the righteous.

He is our Advocate, or the one who pleads our innocence. We aren't innocent because we didn't sin. We are innocent because we are in Him. The Bible says that on the account of sin, Jesus defeated sin in the flesh.[58] His victory is your gift. Sin remains in the flesh, but when we are walking by faith, we are in the Spirit where sin, the law, and the flesh have no power.

If you trust the Bible and begin walking in these things, you will see sin beginning to lose its grip on your life. Each time you stumble, it is a reminder that you have stepped into the flesh. Confess your faith in Christ, step into faith in the Spirit, and leave the flesh behind. It has no power, no rights, and no condemnation against you.

At first it may be a struggle, but as you learn to walk as a believer, spiritual maturity will blossom and sinful tendencies will fall away. One day you'll see something that once plagued you, and

---

[58] Romans 8:3

you'll realize that desire is gone. The flesh still craves it, but because you are no longer led by the flesh, it won't matter.

Sin dwells in the flesh. As you learn to walk by faith, you will be abiding where sin cannot go. It can only beckon from a distance. The habits and tendencies you are now fruitlessly wrestling to escape from will soon fall away as you learn to rest in Christ.

What amazing promises we have been given!

Discussion Questions

Explain what the Apostle Paul meant when he said, "In me nothing good dwells," and "How to perform what is good I do not find."

Why do atheists do good? Can my good deeds come from the same source as that of unbelievers? Explain.

What did Paul mean when he said, "I labored more abundantly than them all, yet not I, but the grace of God which was with me?"

Read 2 Corinthians 5:21. If I am producing my own righteousness, does this make me a rival of Christ?

Which is worse, self-righteousness or lust? Explain.

Review Romans 10:4. When does the law come to an end? For whom does this apply?

Explain why the person exempt from the law wouldn't be led into sin.

What part of our old lives were bound by the law?

What part of our new lives in Christ are still subject to the law?

Why did God make His presence a place of dread in the Old Testament, but then calls it a place of grace and help in the New Testament?

Are you under condemnation if you sin or live according to the flesh?

What does it mean to rest in Christ?

Renewing Your Mind

There are two main hindrances that prevent Christians from experiencing the victorious Christian life. The single most common problem is what we have been discussing. It's ignorance of the difference between the life of the Spirit and living according to the flesh. It's Christians trying to obtain in their flesh the life that can only be experienced in the Spirit.

The second biggest problem in the life of the Christian is neglecting God's call for renewal. A Christian who is not consistently renewing their mind will have an inconsistent spiritual walk, and will be drawn into the flesh more than they will walk in the Spirit.

We've already looked at the Bible's explanation that the flesh wars against our minds, trying to draw us back into the deeds of the old nature. The nature itself is dead, but the deeds continue to live in the flesh.[59] The body desires what the sinful nature once cherished, but we have a new nature that desires the things of God. Yet if our minds are in the flesh, we will begin to live according to the old ways again. Let's begin this chapter by reviewing this important principle. **Romans 8:5-8**

> [5] For those who live according to the flesh set their minds on the things of the flesh, but those *who live* according to the Spirit, the things of the Spirit.
> [6] For to be carnally minded *is* death, but to be spiritually minded *is* life and peace.
> [7] Because the carnal mind *is* enmity against God; for it is not subject to the law of God, nor indeed can be.
> [8] So then, those who are in the flesh cannot please God.

In the flesh, you cannot please God. Remember when we looked at Hebrews 11:6? Without faith it is impossible to please God? Unless you are walking by faith, you *are* walking in the flesh.

---

[59] Romans 6:6, Colossians 3:9

Yet when we are looking to God, He rewards us for diligently seeking Him. By faith, we know these promises are real, therefore, we are seeking God knowing we will receive all we need. His Spirit causes our outward lives to be transformed according to His inward working. The person who doesn't believe this will attempt to transform themselves by outward behavior and outward regulations instead of looking to the Spirit of God that now abides in us.

Even when we understand this truth, we have a problem. We live in a body of flesh and are surrounded by a world that lives for the flesh. In John 13, Jesus finished the last supper and begins to prepare the disciples for His departure. The first thing Jesus does is wash their feet. Two truths emerge from this act. The main point was to show that the Christian life is a life of humility, and even those with a higher status, if they understand the life of faith, will be willing to serve in ways that seem to undermine social hierarchies.

It's something that emerged during this washing that unveils a truth that applies to this study. When Jesus approached Peter, a battle against pride begins. First, Jesus the Lord of all should not be doing the work of a slave. In that culture, people wore sandals and walked along dusty roads. When they reached a destination, the lowest ranking servant would have the task of washing the filth off the guest's feet.

There were no servants at the last supper, and none of the disciples wanted to condescend to this task, so Jesus humbled Himself to do the washing. Peter had two objections to this. First, Jesus should not be doing it. Second, it was hard for him to receive Jesus' humility as a gift. Pride is a funny thing. It doesn't want to serve, and often it doesn't want to receive. Receiving indicates an inadequacy on our part, and it sometimes takes just as much humility to receive as it does to give.

This interaction with Jesus created the opportunity for Him to reveal yet another truth that applies to the topic of this book. First Peter said, "You will not wash my feet." When Jesus warned that he would have no part with Christ unless he submitted. Peter then went to the other extreme. "Then wash my hands, head, and the rest of me."

Jesus answered, "He who is washed needs not to be cleaned, except his feet."

The magnitude of that one statement goes unnoticed by most people. Later that night Jesus will tell His disciples, "You are already clean because of the word I have spoken to you." This truth is later echoed in **1 Corinthians 6:11**

And such were some of you. But you were washed, but you were sanctified, but you were justified in the name of the Lord Jesus and by the Spirit of our God.

If you are in Christ, you are already clean. You have been washed. You have been sanctified, justified, and are now clean. Yet you still walk down the dusty road of life and need to have the parts that are in contact with the world washed. You are clean, but your feet will get dirty. Your goal is to wash away what you are picking up from the world. You do not need to be re-cleansed.

Most Christians approach life like Peter, thinking they must be re-cleansed and are ignorant of the fact that they have been washed. They don't believe the promise, you have been cleansed by the word. You have been washed. You are clean everywhere and only your feet need to be washed.

Peter, through ignorance of the reality of his cleansing, declared, "Not just my feet, but wash everything." Jesus refused. When you don't acknowledge His cleansing and demand to be rewashed, He still refuses.

People are saying, "Not *my* feet," while they are covered by the clinging dirt of this world. Then when they realize the world's filth is creeping in still neglect the call for renewal. Instead they try to be re-forgiven, rewashed, re-cleansed, and never understand the power of God and how He offers to wash their feet daily. They are distracted from the power of renewal by both the deception of sin and by religious misconceptions.

You live in a corrupt world. You must walk down the dusty roads of life. No matter how carefully you walk, how much you try to tiptoe around the things you want to avoid, and how much you abstain from the things you know are harmful, you will get your feet dirty. It's impossible not to be affected by this world. You can't drive down the highway without seeing seductive ads on billboards, hearing worldly conversations at work, and being exposed to sin in daily life. You cannot avoid getting your feet dirty. Your soul will pick up dirt. And this will affect how you think. A life that neglects renewal will begin to conform to the world. Consider this command in **Romans 12:2**

> And do not be conformed to this world, but be transformed by the renewing of your mind, that you may prove what *is* that good and acceptable and perfect will of God.

You will lose the ability to discern the will of God as your mind begins to conform to the world. Your natural mind is part of this fallen world. Each day is a call for renewal. It is impossible to stay spiritually minded without consistent renewal.

In the book of Ephesians, the church is instructed on this very thing. They are warned that the world pursues the things that are sinful and contrary to a life of faith. It goes down the obvious things that are affecting the church through the community around them, and then it gives the solution. Look at **Ephesians 4:20-24**

> [20] But you have not so learned Christ,
> [21] if indeed you have heard Him and have been taught by Him, as the truth is in Jesus:
> [22] that you put off, concerning your former conduct, the old man which grows corrupt according to the deceitful lusts,
> [23] and be renewed in the spirit of your mind,
> [24] and that you put on the new man which was created according to God, in true righteousness and holiness.

The old man or old nature once lived for sin, but the conduct of this nature remains in the flesh. The world appeals to the flesh and since we live in the world, we need something to refocus our minds on eternity. We put off this former conduct (pleasing the flesh) by renewing ourselves in the spirit of our minds.

The Bible says that the mind on the flesh only produces the things of death, but to be spiritually minded is life and peace. [60] Through our time of renewal, we intentionally put off our fleshly way of thinking and put on our new life we have in Christ. Or as the Bible says, "Since we live in the Spirit, let us also walk in the Spirit."[61]

How then do we renew our minds? Let's bring in **Colossians 3:9-10**

> [9] Do not lie to one another, since you have put off the old man with his deeds,
> [10] and have put on the new *man* who is renewed in knowledge according to the image of Him who created him,

We are renewed in knowledge of Christ. To understand this more fully, let's revisit the passage that began this book, **Ephesians 1:17-19**

> [17] That the God of our Lord Jesus Christ, the Father of glory, may give to you the spirit of wisdom and revelation in the knowledge of Him,
> [18] the eyes of your understanding being enlightened; that you may know what is the hope of His calling, what are the riches of the glory of His inheritance in the saints,
> [19] and what *is* the exceeding greatness of His power toward us who believe, according to the working of His mighty power

This is the power of renewal. The Bible says that scripture gives good doctrine (teaching), rebukes what is in error, corrects our way, and gives instruction in the right way. [62] As I learn from the word, I learn what has value, and by this, I can also understand the need to remove what has no value. I learn to look to the Spirit through the eyes of my spirit, and then I receive the knowledge of Him. Then my eyes are opened, my understanding is enlightened,

---

[60] Romans 8:6
[61] Galatians 5:25
[62] 2 Timothy 3:16

and I discover the hope of His calling. That is when I see the richness of His glory and our inheritance.

But wait; there's more. His power is then revealed to me and manifested within me, and that is when I have the power to overcome. I don't have to worry about sin. Sin has no significance once I'm walking in the Spirit. It has no power, for it cannot overcome God's power.

Once you are walking in the Spirit by faith, you are walking according to His mighty power and the flesh has no strength, no value, and no significance. This is the victory that overcomes the world, our faith. That means, if you are walking by faith, you have nothing to overcome. You are now walking in His power, which has already overcome.[63] You are already an overcomer in Christ. You are more than a conqueror.[64]

The world calls, shows you its best offerings, and demands you to participate. If you are in the Spirit, none of these things will move you. But if you neglect renewing your mind, the constant warring of sin will begin drawing you into a fleshly way of thinking, and once your mind is in the flesh, you'll be back into the lamentation of the Apostle Paul, "Though I want to do good, how to perform that good I cannot find."

You will never find the power to do good or overcome unless you are walking by faith. The world bombards you with distractions from Christ, but renewal puts your focus on Christ as it reveals the depth of God's revelation. Then you will see how much there is to explore in Christ.

The Christian life is not a life of monotony. It can be — if you limit yourself to only what you can glean from others. Many very good teachers proclaim the truth in amazing ways, but they can only provide glimpses of what they are discovering. They may indeed be consuming the word, but you are only getting what they can regurgitate back out. And that is limited at best.

The average Christian learns all they will ever learn within three years of being in the church. Most denominational teaching

---

[63] John 16:33, 1 John 5:4
[64] Romans 8:37

Renewing Your Mind

rehashes the same doctrines over and over, and within a few years they are mixing and matching what has already been taught. I say denominational teaching, but this is also true in churches that label themselves as non-denominational.

If you are not seeking the depths of God through personal study and renewal, you'll have a stunted Christian life. But this does not have to be. Take to heart the words of **Romans 11:33**

Oh, the depth of the riches both of the wisdom and knowledge of God! How unsearchable *are* His judgments and His ways past finding out!

You will never discover all that God is waiting to reveal. The deepest Christians are merely just below the surface of God's revelation.

Most Christians bob on the surface, never discovering the depth of God's word. When someone discovers faith, they often fall into the trap of thinking they have arrived. All has been discovered. In reality, each revelation of the word is only the doorway into a world of new understanding. As you learn to go deeper, you'll wonder why you were satisfied with treading on the surface.

Some Christians seem to be so deep, but when you understand the depths of God's word, even the deepest among us are still close to the surface. Here's a word picture. Think about swimming in the ocean. The world record for free diving (diving without gear) is 531 feet. That is an amazing depth. The world record for diving with gear is 1,043 feet. If we look down, this seems incredibly deep. Yet if we pull back and look at the depths of the ocean, these people would still appear to be near the surface.

The Mariana Trench is more than 36,000 feet deep. That means the deepest dive in history has not even reached 3% of the depth of the ocean. A mere feeble attempt.

Now consider the infinite God we serve. Even those who seem to be deep spiritual thinkers are only beginning to discover all that God waits to reveal. Think about how much there is to explore on this earth. Then the awe-inspiring universe our modern era has discovered exists. How much more is out there? We'll never know. Yet even what we know exists is beyond our ability to fully explore, yet how many people find joy in these discoveries?

We have eternity to discover the depths of God and His creation, but the Christian is already standing in eternity. Don't deprive yourself of the joy of what God wants to reveal to you now. Don't merely look at renewal as a way to survive the world. It is also an invitation to discover the revelation of God's word.

The word of God is like peering into the universe. We know there is much that can never be seen with human eyes, but God has given us this part of eternity to explore now. What's more is that we get to bring our discoveries into our lives now so that we can begin living in eternity while waiting for the unveiling of the spiritual world that will be.

When you came to Christ, there was an explosion of joy at this new life you found. Most people stop there, after all, they found life. What they don't realize is that they have entered a life of discovery. There is always joy in discovering new things in God's word and how it transforms your life. Yet occasionally, you'll make a discovery that is so revolutionary that it produces the same joy you received with Christ. It's like getting saved again.

This is not all God has set aside for you. It is one of the things God has placed for you to find. This is the open door for deeper understanding that will one day lead you to another revelation so enlightening that it will feel like getting saved again. This IS the life of renewal in the word. Don't cheat yourself by thinking you have learned all God wants you to know.

Though we can teach the principles that led others to this discovery, we cannot make people see. People have to seek in order to find. We can't understand the discoveries at 1000 feet until we have passed through the 500 foot view. And you can't make it to 500 feet until you pass through 400 feet. Your depth is never intended to be the end of your search. God never wants you to stop discovering, and as you seek, you will continue to be filled with the revelation of His word and knowledge of Him.

Certainly the Bible tells us that we are washed with the water of God's word,[65] but that washing is so we can enter into the house of discovery. God doesn't want you to stop at saying, "Look how clean my feet are," He wants you to feel clean, but also to begin walking with Him and learning to be enriched through the word.

God's word is the truth that washes us, but it is also the revelation of God to us. God is revealing His will, His promises, and your place in Him. And revelation only comes to those who walk in the Spirit, for the word of God can only be discerned through the Spirit.[66]

Don't let this world or your life in the flesh rob you of the richness of God. Don't neglect the word and become fleshly minded. Don't let religion – even Christian religion – keep you busy with meaningless things. Don't limit your spiritual knowledge to only what people can teach – some of which is well meaning but misses the heart of God's intent. Even perfect teaching cannot reveal all God has for you.

Remember, the Bible says that you don't need a person to teach you, for you have the anointing of the Holy Spirit upon you and you know all things.[67] You have all the knowledge available to the believer within the scriptures and the Spirit who resides in you. The only thing lacking is your trust in the Holy Spirit.

God did not limit His revelation to the experts. God does not have a special anointed class. According to the Bible, anyone who teaches such a thing is trying to deceive you.[68] It is God's will for you, the everyday Christian, educated or uneducated, clergy or layman, denominational or non-denominational, it is His will for you to discover His depths by direct revelation by His Spirit through His word. Or as **Jeremiah 33:3** puts it:

> Call to Me, and I will answer you, and show you great and mighty things, which you do not know.'

---

[65] Ephesians 5:26
[66] 1 Corinthians 2:14
[67] 1 John 2:20, 1 John 2:27
[68] 1 John 2:26-27

Be renewed. Seek. Discover. God is already revealing His word to you. Are you listening?

Discussion Questions

"To be carnally minded is death." Does this mean we lose our life in Christ if we set our minds on the things of the flesh? Explain.

Read John 13:9-11. What did Jesus mean, you are clean?

Why did Jesus exclude Judas from the declaration that they were clean?

Why are we unable to discern the will of God?

How much of God's revelation can you receive from teachers, books, and preachers?

What does the phrase 'revelation knowledge' mean to you?

Have you ever felt that your spiritual life or growth in the knowledge of God has stagnated?

Why do people quit growing?

What happens to the life that stops growing?

Are we dependent on teachers in order to know God?

Why did God appoint teachers and church leaders?

Explain what it means to renew your mind.

The Abundant Life

Look at church life around you. Look at the spiritual depth of the average church member. Why are so few people walking in victory? Few Christians believe in the finished work of Christ. We believe Jesus died for our sins, but do we believe the promise that we have been given all things that pertain to life and godliness? Do we believe we are the righteousness of God in Christ? Do we believe we have died to what we were once held by and are now raised in a new life where all things are of God? Do we believe this basic promise, **Ephesians 1:6**

> To the praise of the glory of His grace, by which He has made us accepted in the Beloved.

Do you believe you are accepted solely because you are in the Beloved Son of God? Most Christians struggle to believe God's promises beyond salvation, so they step out of the life of promise and back into a system that is again dependent upon the flesh instead of one that is dependent upon Christ alone. I'll say again, if the weakness of the Law was the flesh, the strength of grace cannot be the flesh. The message of the gospel is that you cannot measure up to God's perfect nature and character; therefore, God fulfilled the law on your behalf, and when you trust in Christ, you are credited with His works as though they are your own.

On the cross, Jesus became your failures, sins, and inadequacies, not because He was inadequate, but that He might bear the shame of your sins and weaknesses and take them out of the way. Then when you believe on Him, all you were was put upon Him and you become what He was in this world. Meditate on **1 John 4:17-19**

> [17] Love has been perfected among us in this: that we may have boldness in the day of judgment; because as He is, so are we in this world.
>
> [18] There is no fear in love; but perfect love casts out fear, because fear involves torment. But he who fears has not

been made perfect in love.

[19] We love Him because He first loved us.

Not only do we believe in the love He has for us, but we receive the promise, "As He is, so are we in this world." You have the life of Christ, but you can walk as a defeated Christian. You can have the abundant life and still live as a spiritual pauper. Or you can walk in faith where the promises are already yours.

Many, if not most, Christians don't believe the promise that sin has been taken out of the way, so instead of walking in the Spirit by faith, they are wrestling against sin in the flesh. They don't believe the promise of God that we have been given all things through Christ, so they are pursuing empty doctrines that lead them away from what they already have been given in Christ. For this reason they are looking to ordinances as a merit system. This type of Christian strives fruitlessly to gain what they don't understand they already possess.

God never blesses that effort, for God will not use you to accomplish what Christ has already accomplished. God does not bless our efforts to make our righteousness a rival to the righteousness of Christ.

We should not be trying to discover how to obtain life in the Spirit or trying to overcome. We must approach the Christian life from the position of victory and receive as people who already have what God promised. God's promises are given in order to reveal His expressions of love / grace. This is not only the eternal life to come, but also the gifts of God already given to us.

The Bible says you have been given all things through Christ and all depends on God's divine power, not our efforts.[69] If you have been given all things that pertain to life and godliness, what do you need to obtain in order to thrive in this Christian life? Nothing. But if you don't understand God's gift, then you'll turn to religious practices and rules as you attempt to gain by human effort what God has already provided by promise.

---

[69] 2 Peter 1:3

God will never allow you to accomplish on your own what He has already accomplished for you. You can never earn what God has given. You can never achieve what Christ has accomplished. To attempt any of these things is a denial of Christ. What's more, when you present your righteousness to God, you are making yourself a rival of Christ. So even if you could produce righteousness, it still would not be accepted, for it is rooted in the pride of the flesh instead of faith in Him.

You need not strive to produce righteousness, for a human life cannot produce spiritual gifts.

Let me reiterate this important truth. The Bible says that the weakness of the flesh is why the law failed in the Old Testament. It is certain that the flesh could never have the strength to support grace by faith in the New Testament. What the law could not do in that it was weak through the flesh, God did by sending His son, Jesus Christ.[70]

The only way to experience life in the Spirit is by trusting completely in Christ. The ONLY hindrance in your life is disbelief. You've probably heard that your sins prevent you from experiencing fellowship with God, but this is false. Read and meditate on **Romans 6:6-7**

[6] knowing this, that our old man was crucified with *Him*, that the body of sin might be done away with, that we should no longer be slaves of sin.
[7] For he who has died has been freed from sin.

You have been freed from sin! It no longer has power over you. It can no longer bring you under bondage. Sin cannot defeat the person living by faith, and it certainly can't overcome the work of Christ.

If you still have the nagging doubt that grace is a license to sin, go back and reread the scriptures we discussed earlier. Sin is ONLY in the flesh, but you ARE in the Spirit. Sin only has the power you submit to it. And the promise is, if you come to your senses and realize you have submitted back under sin, the solution is simple.

---

[70] Romans 8:3

The Abundant Life

Rejoice with the Apostle Paul, "I thank God through Jesus Christ!" When you're in the flesh, you are always serving sin – even if it looks good or masquerades as righteousness. In the Spirit of your mind, you are always serving righteousness.

The life of faith is to learn how to walk according to our new life in Christ. Faith in God's grace cannot lead a person into sin. To say that grace / hyper-grace /complete trust in grace causes people to sin is a blasphemous statement. People believe this lie ONLY because they are looking at grace through the mind stuck in the flesh.

Do you believe the promise, "Old things have passed away and all things have become new?" Do you believe you are a new creation, as the Bible states? If you are a new creation, that new life is of God, in God, and for God. Your new life, by nature, serves righteousness. That new nature is created by God with the same desires as God. That new nature does not need the law, it thrives in righteousness.

The law was written for the flesh. The Bible says the law arouses the flesh and produces the work of death in our bodies.[71] The law does not produce righteousness,[72] it makes us exceedingly sinful.[73] So anyone submitting to the law are not only turning back to the flesh, but they are arousing sin and are certain to experience defeat.

Instead, we have escaped the law by dying to our old sinful nature, being born into a new nature, and now we are learning how to walk according to that new nature whose life is in Christ. We don't turn back to the rules and ordinances, for these only take our eyes off Christ. And when your eyes are off Christ, you are in the flesh. You are either walking by faith and trusting in grace, or you are walking according to your own power to serve the flesh.

Rather than grace creating apathy or excusing sin, grace teaches us to deny ungodliness, for we are focused on the Spirit,

---

[71] Romans 7:5
[72] Romans 3:20
[73] Romans 7:13

where sin cannot go. We are denying the body's demands to turn away from Christ to serve sin. How can this produce sin?

Don't live an unbelieving life. Experience the life and peace of God's promises. Sin has been defeated so you can walk in freedom through the Spirit. It is a lifestyle of faith. And when you blow it, and you will, look again to God's promises, rejoice in what Christ has done, and walk by faith in the promise that you have been set free from sin and free from the law that exposes and condemns sin.

If you want to know more about this topic, it's covered in detail in *Abounding Grace*, so I won't cover it here. What I will reiterate is that you are free so you can pursue your life in the Spirit without distraction.

God doesn't want you to focus on sin. He wants you to focus on Christ. He wants you to believe His word. People will teach many doctrines that deny God's promises, and the reason is because God's word doesn't make sense to the human mind. How can we sin and still be acceptable to God? Isn't this making light of sin? Won't this make people want to sin more? You'll hear many accusations such as this, but let's let Jesus' words explain. **Matthew 13:44-46**

> [44] Again, the kingdom of heaven is like treasure hidden in a field, which a man found and hid; and for joy over it he goes and sells all that he has and buys that field.
> [45] "Again, the kingdom of heaven is like a merchant seeking beautiful pearls,
> [46] "who, when he had found one pearl of great price, went and sold all that he had and bought it.

The world looks at sin as though it's a treasure. A man in destitute poverty will dive into a dumpster and rejoice when he finds trash he can use. But would a wealthy man think his find was a treasure? No. In fact, someone threw away what he now thinks is a treasure. This is sin to the world. It looks good ONLY because they have not discovered the true treasure of life in the Spirit.

I'll take it a step further. A religious man or woman fills their life with do's and don'ts. They rejoice when they attain to any level of spiritual success. Yet a person who is a receiver of Christ looks at that same success and realizes it's trash. And when the religious community realizes a spiritual man or woman no longer values the religion they still cling to, the one who is a receiver of Christ will look like an offender. They will be called 'unspiritual' even though they are the one who has discovered the true life of the Spirit.

Many such people have discovered the life of faith and realized all they valued was worthless. Then they gladly sold their religion and laid hold of life. Like the man finding the treasure in the field, all their possessions become worthless in light of the immense value of what they have discovered. That man sells everything to buy the field so he can obtain that treasure.

What do you think others will say? You've worked your whole life for this stuff. How can you cast it all away? We have this very example in the life of the Apostle Paul.

Paul was a Pharisee. When we think of Pharisees, we think of pompous and arrogant people who hated Jesus. While knowledge does puff up and leads them to reject the humble ways of God, many Pharisees were sincere and thought they were serving God. Paul studied under the most respected teachers of his day. He was on the fast track to success. His entire life was dedicated to religion. And it was a form of religion that came directly out of the scriptures.

Do you know why the religious leaders of the first century missed God? They used the scriptures, but they could not see that everything pointed to faith in Christ. Because they looked at the scriptures as something they must do, they missed the reality of what Christ was doing, and then after His crucifixion, they missed what He has done.

Even those Jews who became Christians struggled to understand the magnitude of what Jesus had done. They believed Jesus paid for their sins, but then they looked at the rest of the scripture as what they had to do for God. The more they looked at scripture outside of faith in Christ, the more they fell into religion and ceased experiencing the fullness of God.

This is why the Bible says to the church of Galatia:

¹ O foolish Galatians! Who has bewitched you that you should not obey the truth, before whose eyes Jesus Christ was clearly portrayed among you as crucified? ² This only I want to learn from you: Did you receive the Spirit by the works of the law, or by the hearing of faith? ³ Are you so foolish? Having begun in the Spirit, are you now being made perfect by the flesh? **Galatians 3:1-3**

Are you so foolish, having begun in the Spirit are you now being perfected through the flesh? The same message echoes down to our day. People came into this church and taught that they are saved by grace, but now they must serve God by keeping the law (rules and practices) by human effort. And the Bible says, "You have fallen from grace."[74]

Have you fallen from grace? Do you know what the solution is? It is to turn back to grace. Trust again in the completed work of Christ and walk in the Spirit. The same faith that brought you salvation is the same faith that perfects you.

Once Paul recognized this truth, he looked at all his accomplishments, education, works, and everything that once held value and said, "I count it all as trash."[75] Everything he worked for was actually loss. Yet many people in his circle didn't accept his change. He became persecuted by those who valued religion, and they hated his teaching that everything is by Christ, through Christ, and is only the work of Christ.

Do you see this problem in the church today? When a life-long church member has spent their whole lives doing the works they have been told they must do to please God, and someone says, "If it's human effort, it's worthless," what do you think they will say? If Joe the deacon has done all the church works believing that he is earning a mansion in heaven, and has been taught that his reward will be based on how much he works, how do you think Joe will react to the Bible's teaching that human effort means nothing?

---

[74] Galatians 5:4
[75] Philippians 3:8

Someone who has invested their lives in religion will be very hostile to the true gospel message, for it undermines all merit systems. No one wants to be told that all their labors are valueless. But here is the good news. It doesn't matter how much of your life you have wasted. God does not measure your life based on how long you have been in faith, but whether you are in faith.

Jesus told a parable about men laboring in a field. In the morning, a land owner hired people to work in his field. He returned at noon and found other people. He sent them to work in the field. One hour before the work day was to end, he took a trip to town and found men idle. He said, "Go and work for one hour, and I'll pay you what I decide."

When he paid the laborers, he gave those who were working for one hour the exact same wage as those who labored all day long. The reason? "I am good, and I will pay the last the same as the first." It was all about grace.

Religion teaches us to labor in the dumpster where nothing good can be harvested. People who have lived in the dump don't understand that even its treasures are worthless to the Kingdom of God. Yet the Bible says that grace creates in us a zeal for good works.[76] However, we are not laboring to obtain our reward. We are yoked with Christ in fellowship as He bears the load and we labor with Him. Though we are laboring, the Bible says, "You who are weary, take My yoke upon you and I will give you rest. For my burden is light."

A yoke is a device that connects two oxen together so they can plow a field. How can we be yoked for work, and be at rest? Because the work is His work, and the labor is God working through us – not us toiling fruitlessly for Him. The one pulling their own plow will never produce fruit. Yet those who answer the call of faith, even in the last hour, are rewarded – not for the wages of their labors, but because God is good.

You must also decide between the dumpster of the flesh and the riches of Christ. Life in the flesh is living for the dump. Some things in the dumpster appear to be good. In every trash heap there

---

[76] Titus 2:11-14

is the stench of decomposing garbage, and things that appear good to fleshly eyes. But it's all trash. Blatant sins may stink, but even things that appear valuable are still the trash of this life. They only appear valuable through the eyes that see only the flesh. In the Spirit, none of those things are valuable. You'll count it all as trash – even the things you've worked to accomplish.

In this world they look good, but when you begin to understand God's promise, "I am your exceedingly great reward," the things outside of Him will lose significance. Not only will you stop focusing on your sins, but you'll stop desiring the things that lead you into sin. These things are no longer your concern. It was God's concern, and it was defeated through Christ and taken out of the way.

Why would you dig up the corpse of sin and try to resurrect what Christ has buried? Even if some of sin's deeds emerge in your life, the command is to reckon (account by faith) yourself dead indeed to sin, but alive in Christ. Your sins are indeed dead. You are indeed alive in Christ. Leave the dumpster and walk by faith. If God took sin out of the way and nailed it to the cross, what do you need to do to finish His work?

You have been freed from sin, the flesh has no power, and God has invited you to walk by faith in the Spirit. Then the promise is, "If you walk in the Spirit, you will not fulfill the lusts of the flesh." You don't need to overcome your sins and weaknesses. Once you are walking by faith and your focus is on Christ, they become irrelevant and powerless.

As this book comes to a close, let me reiterate the important truth that God works in your life by revelation. When you read the scriptures, understanding comes by revelation. This is why the natural mind cannot receive the things of God, for they are spiritually discerned.

Neither I, nor anyone else can teach you how to walk in the Spirit. Teaching can explain the principles that lead you to this revelation, but only God can open our eyes. And God does not reveal everything at once, for as Jesus said, "I have many things to teach, but you cannot yet receive it."[77] This principle is explained well in **Hebrews 5:12-14**

> [12] For though by this time you ought to be teachers, you need *someone* to teach you again the first principles of the oracles of God; and you have come to need milk and not solid food.
>
> [13] For everyone who partakes *only* of milk *is* unskilled in the word of righteousness, for he is a babe.
>
> [14] But solid food belongs to those who are of full age, *that is*, those who by reason of use have their senses exercised to discern both good and evil.

You can't present trigonometry to a kindergarten student. They would say, "Those aren't even numbers." The symbols and equations look absurd. No one can learn calculus until they learn algebra. They can't learn algebra until they learn multiplication and division. Multiplication and division is impossible to comprehend to someone who can't add and subtract.

In the same way, you will never discover the deep things of God if you are sitting idly in infancy. Don't think that you have already learned. Don't be so shallow that you don't believe that deeper truths exist. This is why people fight against fully trusting in grace. If they don't understand the basic truths of man's need and God's promises, then grace just doesn't add up. Then they assume that because they have no concept, grace can't really mean I have been given all things. It has to be limited to what I understand, right? We don't really have the mind of Christ, because I don't believe in unlimited knowledge, someone may think. But is this promise empty words? Or is there more than my limited understanding yet to be discover?

God will not overwhelm you with revelation. He also will not reveal what you have not yet been prepared to receive. Most people never mature, but continue to rehash the first principles of God because they are safe, uncontroversial, and require little of the hearer. But if you begin to exercise what you are learning and seek

---

[77] John 16:12

for God's revelation, He will show you new truths in the word that lead you toward a deeper revelation.

It's all in the word, but only can be received through the Spirit.

If all you are looking for is affirmation of what you already know, this book won't be much value to you. On the other hand, this book can never reveal how to walk in the Spirit. God alone can do this. God draws you with a hunger for more, and if you seek and believe the word, God will begin unveiling the truth of scripture. To the person who disbelieves in the revelation of the Spirit or is unwilling to get out of the 3 year cycle of safe teaching, Christianity will remain a shallow religion.

Someone once said their pastor has a book of sermons that they use to preach every message. For twenty years he has only used this book. Do you think he or his congregation will discover the deeper things of God? It's safe. It will avoid criticism. But it is robbing both the preacher and the listener of the treasures of God's richness.

Never stop learning. Never stop seeking. Believe God's word – even when you don't fully understand. Seek with expectation. There was a time when I forced myself to study the Bible, and rarely did I discover anything I didn't already know. I approached the Bible with the idea, "I hope I get something out of this."

Today I no longer think this way. When I open the word, I KNOW I will discover something God is waiting to reveal. I believe God wants to give me of His richness, and I come to the Bible with the expectation of finding. Rarely do I walk away without saying, "Wow!"

This is my prayer for you. God promises to reveal Himself to you. If you believe, you will receive. If you walk by faith, you will walk as a victorious Christian who has a never-ending expectation of God's goodness and revelation.

It is all about Christ. Walk by faith in Him. Be a receiver of His exceeding grace. Begin the lifelong process of learning to walk according to your new nature. Experience the promise of the abundant life!

Discussion Questions

Why do many Christians not live as victorious believers?

What does this mean, "You are accepted in the Beloved?"

What does the Bible mean when it says, "As He is, so are we in this world?"

Explain what it means to be freed from sin.

Can walking in our new nature cause us to sin?

Read Titus 2:11-14. What three things does the Bible say that grace teaches us not to do?

What six things does grace teach us to do?

Read 1 Corinthians 15:10 and review Titus 2:14. Does grace produce apathy?

If grace produces good works, what is the source of works outside of grace?

Will God receive the works He is not producing?

Can someone walk in the Spirit without faith in God's grace?

Can someone walk in the Spirit by fulfilling the law by personal effort?

Why don't people grow beyond shallow faith?

Do you think God rewards you based on how much you do?

What is the abundant life?

Has this book changed your perspective? If yes, in what way?

Other Recent Books by Eddie Snipes

It is Finished! Step out of condemnation and into the completed work of Christ.

The Victorious Christian Life: Living in Grace and Walking in the Spirit.

The Promise of a Sound Mind : God's plan for emotional and mental health

Abounding Grace: Dispelling Myths and Clarifying the Biblical Message of God's Overflowing Grace

Everyday Leadership: The Christian's Guide to Managing Yourself and Others

More books from this author:

- Simple Faith: How every person can experience intimacy with God
- I Called Him Dancer – Christian Fiction
- God Loves the Addict: Experiencing Recovery on the Path of Grace
- Out of the Ashes: How Unplanned Trials Reveal God's Planned Grace
- I Called Him Dancer Christian fiction about God's love for an addict with no hope.

Made in the USA
San Bernardino, CA
28 May 2015